Prepared to Answer

Telling the Greatest Story Ever Told

Mark A. Paustian

NORTHWESTERN PUBLISHING HOUSE
Milwaukee, Wisconsin

Library of Congress Control Number: 2004101360
Northwestern Publishing House
1250 N. 113th St., Milwaukee, WI 53226-3284
© 2004 by Northwestern Publishing House
www.nph.net
Published 2004
Printed in the United States of America
ISBN 978-0-8100-1647-7
ISBN 978-0-8100-2485-4 (e-book)

18 19 20 21 22 23 24 25 26 27   18 17 16 15 14 13 12 11 10 9

CONTENTS

Introduction

Christ in Prophecy

The Arrival of God

The Ministry of Jesus

Our Lord's Passion

Resurrection and Ascension

The Christian Church

Conclusion

INTRODUCTION

"What story?"

Impromptu speeches. Remember those? I do. I recall one time drawing a slip of paper from the hat that read "Boxing." In the time it took me to walk to the front of my Dale Carnegie class (and a person can only walk so slowly), I had to decide what in the world I wanted to say in a speech about boxing. But in that class the teacher offered one magical piece of advice: Think of a personal story relating to whatever it said on the slip of paper.

So, when I reached the front, I turned around and told a story of the boxing matches that occurred between my brother Phil and me when we were kids. Our boxing "ring" was a blanket spread on the bedroom floor. Our "gloves" were two pairs of socks pulled over our fists. The only rule was, "Don't hit too hard." (I didn't say we were bright.) And a vivid memory of the two of us inevitably rolling around on the ground, mad as hornets, turned into a poignant lesson about the big brother you fought with while your parents sighed and told you he'd be important to you one day. I know that if I could go back, I would try not to hit so hard. (Not bad, for 20 seconds' notice.)

When it comes to speaking off the cuff, without preparation, how liberating it is to change the question from, What in the world do I have to say about that? to, Quick . . . what story can I tell? And that's where the premise for this book was born. It is an idea that has completely changed how I look at impromptu speaking on the topic of my Christian faith.

What story can I tell?

As I write, I'm relishing a conversation from just two days ago. A woman I had just met, named Kayla, was cutting my hair. I had a Christian book in my lap (which all by itself can start some interesting conversations), and she began telling me about the fights between her parents, actual physical fights, that she had witnessed when she was just eight or nine years old. She would get in the middle of them, if you can imagine what that was like. But what she remembers most from that time in her life was how a man once came into her room in the middle of the night and sat on the side of her bed. She could just make out his face. She's convinced it was Jesus.

Here her story broke off. She remembered her scissors and what was left of my hair. It was my turn. What should I say? What would you have said?

What would you have to say about a boxing match between a mom and dad? More important, what would you say to a woman who hides such a tentative faith in her heart and who has been waiting 20 years for someone to come along and explain this man to her? Do you say, "Let me tell you about a program we have at our church"? Do you give her a list of worship times? What in the world do you say? No, change that. What story do you tell?

You know, Jesus did go to a little girl in her bed. Did you know that?

No.

And I told the story about the concerned dad who was rich but would have given it all away for his sick little girl.

"Let's go to her," Jesus said.

But they got delayed, helping someone else along the way. The father's heart was breaking. Then the news came that it was too late.

"I'm afraid I've wasted your time," the father said to Jesus.

"No. No, you haven't. She's only sleeping."

I paused to ask if she had heard this story before. She had not and was clearly interested. So I told her the whole thing, right up to *"Talitha Koum,"* which means, "Little girl, get up!"

And she did.

Kayla, I believe Jesus still comes to people who are dead—dead inside because they don't know love and they don't know God; they only have shame. God wants them to be alive and not be afraid, so he comes to them in his Word. The one who died on the cross for them draws near, saying: "Be of good cheer. Your sins are forgiven." And when people hear his voice in those words—when they only believe him—they live.

It was a remarkable conversation. In the most natural way, it traveled from there to the prayer Jesus prayed in the Garden of Gethsemane, then to the moment Jesus turned his head away from the gall they offered him at his crucifixion, and at last to the upper room where the disciples gathered to grieve and to be ashamed and to figure out what they were going to do without Christ. After his resurrection, Christ's first words to them were, "Don't be afraid." All this I told Kayla.

And out of the suffocating fog of religion stepped her Savior.

There is power in the words and deeds of Christ to show us the evil in ourselves, power to smash apart our godforsaken complacency and to reveal our desperate need for his grace. Even more, according to the apostle John, "These [words] are written that you may believe that Jesus is the Christ, the Son of God, and that by believing you may have life in his name."[1]

Through the use of divinely inspired narratives such as this, we give people something they'll remember, something that gains entrance to their minds and that will stay with them, even when they don't yet understand it. This is what it means to plant a seed. Something alive and waiting is hidden in the shell of the story.[2] The people don't know what it is or what it means. And then, one day . . . they do.

"Little girl, get up!"

As a pastor and professor, I face challenging situations all the time. I walk into a room where someone has just died, or is about to. I'm invited into a marriage where something shameful has just been exposed. I see grown men cry because they're about to fail and don't know one thing they can do to stop it. And I get questions and challenges from intelligent and hurting people who are skeptical that there is a God somewhere loving them. You will find yourself in these situations too. If you don't, just carry a book with the word *Jesus* in the title to your next hair appointment.

These situations used to fill me with apprehension because I never felt prepared. Now just about every situation I can think of suggests to me a story that I can't wait to tell. For several years my study of the Scriptures has meant collecting moments and words from the life of Jesus, the ones that especially move me, the ones that reveal God to me and clarify the big issues of my life. More and more I've been marrying these beautiful stories to all kinds of situations and questions that I'm likely to face in a world that sorrows under the long shadow of death. This has been my preparation.

Let the woman who wonders if God can really forgive her listen to the stones of accusation thudding in the dirt and the impossible words Jesus spoke to a woman caught in the act of adultery. "I don't condemn you."

Let the man struggling with doubt watch Peter sink under the waves. He was not walking on the water. All he could muster was a panicky "Lord, save me." It was enough. "Jesus reached out and caught him."

And what a holy pleasure to take people so terrified of death to the entrance of a first-century grave where a woman stood by and softly shed the tears of all the world. Her Lord was dead. She had nothing else, because there is nothing else . . . until one word turned her utterly around. He said, "Mary."

My prayer is that this marriage of skeptical questions with well-loved gospel stories might be your preparation as well. May you become more and more familiar with the magnificent, true story God lived in this world through Jesus, his Son, and always more aware of the answers that are alive in him.

Has someone questioned the hope that you have?

Do you want to be prepared to answer?

Then remember that little secret about speaking impromptu. The slip of paper you've drawn says "Jesus."

What story will you tell about him?

A word about this book . . .

I am well aware that the primary audience of this humble book will be Christians. However, you'll find that I've written as if speaking directly to honest-to-goodness skeptics. I've met many such people in my life and have come to care about them. Their faces were before me as I wrote.

My hope is that by writing as if my audience consists of people outside of Christ, this book will be all the more helpful for my Christian readers. These pages, therefore, suggest here and there the actual words you can say to such people and even the spirit with which you might say them.

If you should share actual portions of this book with non-Christians, you'll need to be aware of things that may need further explanation. (Who's Moses? Where is Galilee? Who's Paul?—those kinds of things.) It is a thrill to think you might offer this book to someone who needs it. However, please don't hand this book to a questioning soul as a substitute for the love and truth *you* can offer face-to-face and heart-to-heart.

If any skeptics should happen to read this work to the end, you have my admiration for the integrity of your search for the truth. Sadly, many do not really want to know it. Indeed, left to ourselves, our minds will exhaust themselves in erecting one barrier after another, always saying, "That may be so, *but what about . . . ?*"

If you find yourself asking instead, "Could this really be true?" you may be closer to God than you think.

And he to you.

That would make my joy complete.

In Christian love,
Mark Paustian

"Why Jesus?"

Roughly one thousand years before Christ, the king of Israel wrote a poem about a kingly despair. It begins, "My God, my God, why have you forsaken me?" David wrote as though surrounded by a merciless, mocking crowd. As the painful, poetic words came pouring out, it was as though his bones were being pulled out of joint, as though wounds ran through both his hands and feet, as though an insatiable thirst overcame him while people nearby gambled over his last shred of clothing.

It sends chills.

King David was describing a crucifixion, even though, from his vantage point in history, he had never seen nor heard of one. This is what a crucifixion is like: the bones are pulled out of joint, the hands and feet are pierced, dehydration sets in with the deadly loss of blood. What is more, David was describing the very crucifixion of Christ himself, portrayed ten centuries in advance—the mocking of the crowd, "Let the Lord rescue him if he delights in him"; the gambling for his clothes; the despairing cry from the cross in the center, "My God, why?"

Some seven centuries before Jesus, a prophet named Isaiah gave the Chosen One's name as *Immanuel*, which means "God with us." His mother would be a virgin, the prophecy said, through whom the divine would embrace our humanity. His Father would be God himself.

The prophet Micah chimed in with the birthplace of the Chosen One (being careful to name the right Bethlehem): "From you, Bethlehem Ephrathah, will come one whose origins are from of old." From Moses we learned his family line—a descendant of Judah—and his calling—"a prophet like me." Daniel squarely placed the coming of Christ's eternal kingdom into the glory days of Rome. Had we read the ancient Scriptures, we could have known that wonders would fall from his fingers and brilliant stories from his lips. From the start we would have set our gaze on Galilee and along the Jordan River. One prophet saw him riding into Jerusalem like a king on a donkey. Another set the price of his betrayal at 30 pieces of silver. We could have known it would be a friend who would betray him. We would have heard ahead of time about the shredding of his back as if torn up by a plow, the wine vinegar they would offer him, the surprise of bones left unbroken, the piercing of his side, and even the rich man's tomb where the world's victim would be laid.

David sang the promise that no grave could ever hold the Chosen One.

And Isaiah even told why Jesus was to be led so silent, "like a lamb to the slaughter." "For our transgressions," Isaiah said. "The punishment that brought us peace was upon him, and by his wounds we are healed."

(Please read Isaiah chapter 53.)

It's a daunting task, this book. As I begin my search for words to describe the one I believe in and to put my finger on why I believe, I'm staring at a gruesome photograph. It's the blurry, browning record of the lynching of a black man in Alabama around 1906—his swollen face, his opened yet dead eyes, his bare feet dangling inches above the ugly, gleeful faces that are white like mine. Their racist chins jut forward in mock manhood. They brought along their boys, who are grinning too. The one on the rope doesn't hang there for anything he's done, so much as for who he is.

It's a disturbing picture.

I'm imagining how it would sound to you if I tapped that picture, that swollen face, those dead yet opened eyes, and said, "This is God." You would think the suggestion was absurd. It is absurd that this man might be the awesome Creator—the sort of God who would come into the world for this very rope and this very tree and these very men— that died to redeem us all because he loved us all. Of course, the one Christians believe was God saving the world wasn't a black man from early in the last century, but a Jewish man from a bit further back in history. Does this somehow make that belief make sense?

No.

I lay this picture side by side with that other death, that other lynching, to remember that it may sound no less absurd when I say such things about Jesus Christ. I turn from that repulsive photograph to a death even more disturbing, more innocent, more vicious, more public, so that while I write of it to you, I am really seeing it myself.

That swollen face, those pierced, naked feet lifted up above the ground—those belong to God? Is there something in me so wrong, so bad, that the only answer to help me is his death? Behind everything my eyes can see there hides an infinite Deity who would do such a thing for me?

I know how it sounds, but what if it were true? And just how might God let us know for sure? What if he wrote about it in excruciating detail before it happened, not rope burns and a tree branch, but pierced hands and a bloody spear?

What if he wrote it into prior history, into the sacred literature and on pages already browning and cracking long before Christ was even born? What if we could read the what, the when, the where, and the how in Scriptures written centuries earlier, the dating beyond dispute? What if we found in those writings not only the who, "God with us," but even the why?

"I will not forget you! See, I have engraved you on the palms of my hands."[3]

Now think of this. Suppose that against staggering odds there was an actual person in history to whom the prophetic signs accidentally pointed. Let's say there was by pure coincidence, early in the first century (not the second), someone in Israel (not India) from Bethlehem (not Bethany) from the line of Judah (not Levi) who was sold out, betrayed, flogged, pierced, and over three hundred "et ceteras." What do you think are the chances that this random person would turn out to be anyone at all or have anything special to say? What if, against one in ten billion odds, this person just happened to be the greatest figure in human history, the one who divides the entire human story into a before and an after? What if these unique prophetic credentials just happened to belong to the one whose miracles were witnessed by thousands; the one of whom observers said, "No one ever spoke the way this man does"[4]; the one whose executors shuddered, "Surely he was the Son of God"[5]; and the one whose resurrection from the dead was the big, bold fact that swept through the world? What if the guns of persecution were held to the temples of those who shouted, "We saw him die, and he met us alive," but they did not shrink back or deny what they saw? What if this man's most outrageous claims— "Heaven and earth will pass away, but my words will never pass away"[6]—insist on coming true, even now in the quiet spot where you sit and read them? What if to this day millions of lives have changed from the inside out just by people believing the news that they have forgiveness through pure grace and are bound for a shimmering glory that can somehow also be called home?

This is what I find: the phenomenon of prophecies that were always right and never wrong; the unimpeachable witnesses to the events of Christ's life, death, and resurrection; and the colossal impact felt around the world and all across time—these lines all converge on a single human being.

I'd like you to meet Jesus.

To seriously compare him with other founders of other faiths is to have a sudden epiphany—there is no one like him. So, I ask you, how does it look to you now, this prophetic portrait of the lynch mob with faces too much like mine and, lifted up in their midst, the black-and-blue face of the Lord of life?

You already know the portrait's title. Read it one more time: "For God so loved the world . . ."

In the earlier part of his life, Charles Templeton, a close friend of Billy Graham, was an evangelist. Yet later on he no longer believed the claims of Christ because of the very issues I'll take up in this book. What is unforgettable about Templeton, however, is the way he still cared about Jesus and the nostalgic way he still spoke of him: "The greatest human being who ever lived . . . the intrinsically wisest person I've encountered . . . the least duplicity, the greatest compassion of any human being in history . . . the most important person ever born. Everything decent I know, I learned from him. There have been many wonderful people, but Jesus is Jesus."

In saying that, his voice began to crack. And his words, just before tears flooded his eyes and his shoulders started to shake, were these: "I miss him."[7]

It lodges sideways in my throat because, in my own way, I miss Jesus too—not the way you miss an imaginary friend or a pleasant dream you used to have, but the way you long for the Savior to come for you at last, so you may see face-to-face the one you found in the Word. You surely will see him. Every prediction was perfect. Every promise came true. There's only one more: "I am coming soon."

Just imagine. If the promise of it is so sweet, what will that day be?

"Amen. Come, Lord Jesus."[8]

"Where is the evidence that God even exists?"

Some say, "This world is all there is. What you grasp with your five senses is the whole story. What you see is all you get." We call them materialists. They believe that nothing exists besides this material world of matter, space, energy, and time. They do not always see that when they banish God to the world of make-believe, they also banish meaning, morality, hope, and even love.

Some people say they're wrong: "There are more things in heaven and earth, than are dreamt of in your philosophy."[9]

There are more.

If God himself once broke the silence of heaven with the four words "Do not be afraid," if he once sent an angel to a nice young girl named Mary, then nothing would ever be the same. Then the materialist world would be the make-believe one. Suddenly, with that one, sparkling, angelic appearance, anything would be possible. We could begin to use the old words again, words like *peace* and *joy.* There would even be a way from here to there, a bridge between all we can see and the So Much More.

Well, guess what? God did. Indeed, God has spoken. He uttered one perfect word. It was the name of a child. Gabriel said to Mary, "You will . . . give birth to a son, and you are to give him the name Jesus."

(Please read Luke 1:26-56.)

I'm picturing you, dear readers, as an audience in an auditorium. The stage in front of you—we'll call it *religion* for lack of a better word—is dark. You're wondering if there is anyone standing on it or if it's as empty as some people think. I sit in the lighting booth somewhere in the back of the auditorium. Before me are the switches to a thousand spotlights trained on that shadowy stage. Making arguments for the existence of our loving, holy God and for the reality of Christ, his Son, is like trying to click these spotlights on, one at a time. The existence and design of the world. Click. The unquiet voice of conscience. Click. The startling phenomenon of prophecy. Click. The unimpeachable eyewitness testimony. Click. And Jesus.

Click. Click. Click.

So many spotlights. So much to be said. I hardly know where to begin. My prayer is that at some point I won't need to turn on another light, advance another argument, and make another point. I will count on the power of God's Word, on the relentless working of his Spirit, and on God's own desire to be known. I remember that Moses didn't find God. God found Moses, drew Moses on wrinkled, bare feet toward a bush that burned and burned, and spoke his own marvelous name: "I AM." So also with me: the reason I believe in God is God.[10] He still finds ways to descend to us, because we are unable to rise to him. Though my words are weak, his grace and power are the reasons I write to you with joy and confidence. The One on the stage can be trusted to reveal himself.

There will always be those who know him. He will see to it. As we merely listen and take his Word to heart, the lights go on. There appears on our stage the figure of a Man with arms stretched wide. Christ is God come searching for what he lost—God come so close as to share our own flesh and blood and everything it means to be us—everything. He died the way he died that we might know him. Through his death he says what he has forever wanted to say: "I love you infinitely. I forgive you completely. I give your life meaning as simply as this: it means something to me. I will take you to a place that can only be called heaven, and this hope from there will stay alive beneath the rubble of every shattered dream here."

In other words, "I can give you God. That is who I AM."

What will your burning bush be? Will you be reading the "Jesus stories" in this book or staring up at the stars? Will you have the gospel of John lying open? Or will you be stroking your little girl's hair when . . . click . . . you suddenly know that He Is? You know because he entered the barren world of the materialist and whispered his name: "I AM."

Now may I reach for the first two switches, namely, two of the classic arguments for the existence of God? One is the "cosmological argument," that is, the reason for the universe. This is the gripping question: Why is there something rather than nothing? Nothingness wouldn't need to be explained. Once there is something, however, we have to ask *why*. Being cannot come from nonbeing. From everything we've ever seen or thought of within the observable universe, whatever begins—whatever did not necessarily have to be—must have a cause. There are no exceptions. A watch found in the woods? Someone made it and left it there. A loud bang at the door? Someone or something is behind it. What of the universe itself? Who is behind it?

I submit that the atheist is not sufficiently amazed by existence itself. And unless you dream that the entire cosmos sprang out of nothingness into existence itself, caused itself, rescuing itself from nonexistence,[11] you must search beyond the realm of matter, energy, space, and time to explain it. Then you come eventually to that one, necessary, eternal, self-existent uncaused cause.

"In the beginning God . . ."[12]

Then there's the "teleological argument," that is, the argument from design. It's a law, not a theory, of science that states that things left to themselves "tend to go from order to disorder." When we observe even the simplest marks of order, let's say we keep finding our M&Ms arranged according to color, our thoughts cannot help but run this way: "Someone is doing this." Someone. What we would never expect blind chance to accomplish, not in a million years, a small child can do in five minutes. Let's, please, just admit what we all know full well: intelligence is a far better explanation for those M&Ms than accident is.

Now consider the dizzying complexity we call life. You can fill a library with facts like these: A living cell contains about two hundred thousand amino acids. The time required for the chance formation of even one—just one!— of the chains of acids found in a living cell can be estimated mathematically, and it is roughly three hundred times the age of the earth according to the evolutionist model (set at 4.6 billion years). The easy appeal that, after all, anything can happen given a long enough amount of time in a big enough universe doesn't hold up under scrutiny.

Have you heard of DNA, the miraculous stuff of life? Each cell of your body has the information for making you; this information would fill an entire library. Information! It's not going too far to say that DNA is actually a message—scientists have recognized that there is "an identity of structure between DNA and written languages."[13]

In his book *Darwin's Black Box,* molecular biologist Michael Behe coined the term *irreducible complexity.* That memorable phrase describes a fact that could not have been known at the time the theory of evolution was spawned, that is, before it was possible to observe life at the molecular level. Throughout your body are countless biological systems consisting of numerous parts that work together with dizzying intricacy—fascinating and complex machines that could not even begin to function if each component of the system was not precisely designed and perfectly in place. Irreducible complexity simply means that no step-by-step process of gradual improvements can possibly account for the mysterious workings of life at the biological level. (Try to imagine a flat piece of wood that catches a few mice . . . when you add a couple staples, it catches a few more . . . then you put a spring under the staples, and it catches even more . . . and as the swinging metal bar gradually evolves to just the right length, the trap just gets better and better at catching mice. This makes sense?) Behe, writing without a hint of religious bias, convincingly suggests that the word *evolution,* when spoken over such intricacies as corneas and flagellums, is more like a magic wand than an explanation. When the biologist peers down a microscope, there's an elephant in the room. The painfully obvious explanation that people somehow manage to avoid is, simply, intelligent design.

Scientists themselves have conceded that the fact that there is an earth in the first place, that there exists this solitary island of life in this "just right" universe, strains faith in blind chance to the breaking point.[14] One astronomer calculated the odds of an island of life forming—based on the necessary forces, properties, and conditions required by a life-sustaining planet—at one in one thousand quintillion, quintillion, quintillion, quintillion, quintillion, quintillion, quintillion.[15] Life as we know it is truly balanced on a razor's edge.

It is not beyond our capabilities to distinguish accident from intelligent design beyond any reasonable doubt. Not only common sense allows us to do that very thing with a high degree of confidence but several disciplines also, including archaeology and forensic science, have clearly articulated the principles involved (not to mention the Carl Sagans of the world who listen for radio signals from outer space). People can maintain all day long that they see no thought or intention hidden behind the marks of incomprehensible order stamped on every flat space in the universe and on their own foreheads. I really think they know better, that's all.

If it were any other question besides the question of origins, so laden with "religious implications" (to quote the grudging admission of Stephen Hawkings), the case would be closed. The possibility that life came about by accident can be effectively ruled out. This explains why when you want to find an atheist for a good, rigorous debate, you go to the philosophy department at the nearest university—the physics and biology departments are getting less helpful all the time. From my point of view, the triumph of materialist assumptions is poised to topple like the Berlin Wall—an apt comparison on several levels.

Now, I suppose the most astronomical of odds can theoretically be overcome—1 in 1 followed by a million zeroes is not technically impossible. Yet, even if coincidence were marginally possible, that misses the point entirely. Would I bet my soul on those odds? Which is the better explanation for the staggering design in our world and in us, blind chance or the intelligence and purpose of a Designer? Can you really stand on a rocky coast at twilight or explore the human marvels of an eye or brain . . . or gaze at your newborn baby . . . and not take it all personally?

"I praise you because I am fearfully and wonderfully made."[16]

Are there no counterarguments that seem plausible to those who have listened? Of course there are. That is the nature of the question—after the argument is made, a person is always left to ask, "Do I accept this?" The answer comes from another place entirely, beyond the realm of reason. Our depraved nature can always find a reason to say no. God himself must utter his own, "I AM."

What is so important to me personally about reasoning from cause and from design (just two among many intriguing arguments) is that I can state these particular cases with utter certainty. The reason I know they are valid and will prevail is that God advanced them first in the Holy Scriptures. "The heavens declare the glory of God; the skies proclaim the work of his hands."[17]

I rest my case on God's own revelation. Reasons for taking the Scriptures to heart will follow in this book, but here I give you my bottom line: I do not call on my best thinking to validate what God's Word has already said. Please notice that I'm working from the other direction. It is God's own Spirit, the author of the Bible, who validates my awe—the appropriate hush as I stare at the fingers of my right hand. When I think of my child "knit together in the secret place" that is my bride's womb and think the self-evident thought, "Someone is doing this," God himself confirms the instinct in his sure Word. I am *sure* that I am right to listen to the song the night sky sings, to look up, and to wonder, not because some philosopher has given me permission to do so, but because . . .

The Bible tells me so.

When Job lost everything he held dear, when his wife, his friends, and his own gut-wrenching pain all argued against God, it was God himself that held the man together. God did that for Job. And he can certainly hold me up—and my faith—by the power of his Word alone, so that "I know that my Redeemer lives."[18] I know.

"Where's the evidence God even exists?" Perhaps this is your bottom line. "Why can't I see him?" Allow me to adapt an analogy made by Christian apologist and Oxford don C. S. Lewis. Consider that expecting to find God in this world as just another visible, material thing like us is like expecting to find William Shakespeare as a character in one of his plays. Look for him this way and the author is nowhere to be found, not in all the skies over fair Verona. But ask again, "Where is Shakespeare in his plays?" He is everywhere—behind every word and letter and in the space between them.

If there were no Shakespeare, there would be no play.

Do you see that God is to this world something like the author is to the play? That is why you could search the entire cosmos and never find his face. And yet the tiniest seed—of a tree or, for that matter, of a man—is a deafening cry: "He Is."

It is just at this point that we confront the real mystery beating at the center of Christianity. The Author did find a way somehow to step inside the tragic play. We needed him to. The Artist did enter his own masterpiece, though the masterpiece was defaced by sin. By a journey we can't fathom—neither its distance nor its cost—God came near, saying, "Do not be afraid."

For nothing, I mean nothing, is impossible with him.

A Russian cosmonaut traveled into space and said, "I didn't find God."

King David knew better. "Where can I flee from your presence? If I go up to the heavens, you are there; if I make my bed in the depths, you are there."[19]

Where can I go and not find God? Where can I run and not hear the unmistakable echo of "I AM"?

Mary finds out she's having a baby. An angel told her.

When this newborn baby comes squirming from the virgin's womb, the heavens themselves open, and the sky fills up with even more angels singing, "Glory!" A star crawls across the expanse and takes its place over God's hometown.

Christmas miracles. Can we believe them? Can the laws of nature be set aside? As Mary put it, "How [can] this be?"

What becomes fairly obvious is that Mary knew where babies come from. Some say that ancient people like Mary believed in miracles because they lived in a "pre-scientific age." Actually, the Bible itself speaks of "miracles, signs and wonders," precisely because people knew enough about the laws of nature to be stunned to see them upset. Two thousand years of advancing knowledge haven't made miracles any more or less wonderful than they already were for Mary.

No less a miracle than the things she heard about is that she believed they would happen.

The truth is, there are laws of human nature that are as dependable as any law of science. We do not naturally trust the things that come from God. We reliably resist him every time, in every way. In this we are as predictable as gravity. The real question is whether the laws of my own nature can be supernaturally set aside. Can God break into my darkness with the miracle of light? Can he interrupt and intervene in the way things naturally go . . . in me?

Just listen to Mary saying, "May it be . . ." and, "My spirit rejoices in God my Savior."

(Please read Luke 1:26-56.)

I need to tell you about my two favorite movies. *Chariots of Fire* is a film about runners in the 1924 Paris Olympics. In *It's a Wonderful Life,* a man sees what the world would be like if he had never been born. Here's the question: How would I feel if the first movie included a miracle, say, angels carrying Eric Liddel across the finish line in the 400-yard run? I would leave the theater thinking, "That was dumb!" I would call it a cheap writer's ploy to reach a happy ending. The miracle doesn't fit.

It's not that kind of movie.

Now think about *It's a Wonderful Life*—an angel appears and a miracle happens to show George Bailey what life would be if he was never born. Do I complain, "Now that's just stupid"? Actually, no. This time the miracle is the pivotal moment—what the whole movie is about. The miracle fits because—how else can I say this?

It is that kind of movie.

I'm trying to put my finger on the reaction some people have to biblical miracles. Are miracles embarrassing? Do they offend thinking people? The whole question of miracles has to do with what kind of "movie," if you will, we are living in. Do miracles fit? Well, just what kind of world is this?

The relevant question is, Do we live in the materialist's world or not? Is what we see all there is, or is there more? If the materialists are right, naturally, miracles are excluded. However, if we simply believe there is more out there than what we can reach with our reason and senses, then we can have no serious problem believing in miracles. Rather than imagining that science has ruled out miracles, it is just as easy to see how a single, authentic miracle is sufficient to shatter the myth of materialism. Miracles are signs that point to something More, and honest people have reported tens of thousands of them.

Whether people acknowledge miracles and the deeper realities they evidence has everything to do with the assumptions they bring to the question. (Skeptic David Hume's classic tests to show that no miracle has ever taken place can also be used to show that Napoleon didn't exist.) If those whose philosophy excludes miracles were to witness one, they would likely doubt their senses rather than their unbelief . . . so that no proof of the miracle is even possible.

But with these words, "In the beginning God . . ."[20] we knew it. It's that kind of world. We were given at the outset a perfectly cohesive explanation to so mysterious a universe as this. We who know Christ, the one "sustaining all things by his powerful word,"[21] understand that if water stays water because he is all the while telling it to, willing it, there is nothing impossible about it becoming wine if he should will that instead. Finally, in the miracles of Jesus' ministry, he was only doing, in his words, "what he sees his Father doing."[22] The Father has been healing bodies and bringing many fish from a few since time began.

You may doubt all this, but not on the basis of good science. Science has nothing important to say about miracles. It has no place even venturing an opinion. Learning always more about natural laws through controlled observation cannot add one thing to the question of whether these laws can be interrupted by something or someone that exists outside of them. And science should not complain too loudly that it has never seen a miracle, for neither has it seen a "Big Bang," nor any small bit of life ever emerge from nonlife, nor any of the most critical processes the theory of evolution requires.

Instead, notice that while I am free to accept or dismiss someone's claim of a miracle based on honest investigation, the atheistic mind is not free. It is made up in advance. It cannot consider the mountain of evidence for miracles objectively. It has a doctrine against miracles.

In this case it is the materialist, not the Christian, who is constrained by a creed.

If one has an *a priori* assumption that the material universe is the whole show, that person has no intellectual freedom but must accept the wildest, most improbable natural explanations. Consider the ultimate miracle on which Christianity entirely depends. Was Christ raised? The materialist mind is forced to believe tales of mass hypnosis and of ten thousand people telling a lie because they enjoyed persecution. That mind is not free to even consider a simple explanation that takes in all the historic evidence, a miracle named Jesus.

Though some would demythologize the Bible, you must understand that a miracle-less Christianity is not possible. While stories of miracles were attached to figures like Buddha and Muhammad centuries after they died, you can strip those miracles away, and the religious beliefs themselves are not affected. Not so with Christianity. The Christian faith does not have miracles tacked on. It *is* miracle. As C. S. Lewis said, the Christian story has been about one "Grand Miracle" from the very start, the miracle of incarnation. God wrapped himself in flesh and blood. As is often pointed out, if the miracle is false, then Christianity itself is of no importance. Ah, but because it is true, nothing in all of human history matters more than the baby named Jesus. This birth was an intrusion into this world by the One who caused all that we see in the first place. This is the pivotal event on which the entire human plot turns. Everything else Christianity claims—that his death would atone for us all, that no grave could hold him down, that eternity is opened wide—follows as a matter of course, if we can get this one question right: Who was that child?

"The holy one to be born will be called the Son of God."[23]

Lastly, before you dismiss the miracles of Jesus as no different from those claimed in the beliefs of any other religion, notice that *his* were performed in public. His were witnessed by thousands, believers and unbelievers alike, and were accepted as fact by his bitterest enemies. Listen to the worries of those Pharisees and priests who hated him the most: "Here is this man performing many miraculous signs. If we let him go on like this, everyone will believe in him."[24]

Indeed.

Best of all, notice how marvelously the miracles do fit. Here are no arbitrary displays designed only to impress, such as Jesus' crude band of fishermen might have invented. See the harmony between the deed and the Man when Jesus straightened a woman's back that had been bent for 14 years or when he whispered to a widow, "Don't cry" and raised her only son. His miracles had to do with reversing the curse of sin. They were promises about the final restoration of all that has gone wrong here—the restoration that rests in his capable, pierced hands. Recognize in the wonders Christ performed what you might call the natural laws of heaven: no one dies here and no one grieves, no one cries here and no one ever hurts. Through the Wonderful Life of Christ, the way things go there broke into here, where we weep and sigh and groan for a little while. By the miracle of the inspired

Scriptures themselves, we have his signs still, and still they point to the living reality of Christ.

Now you may keep asking for empirical evidence when none is inherently possible, as is the case for miracles. You may keep demanding more evidence without bothering to explain just what sort of evidence would convince you, so that the reasons for your denial are not too closely scrutinized. After all, God forbid that you should be duped, that you should reach for the miraculous too quickly.

But is there no mistake to be made in the other direction?

Many people miss "the big facts"[25] in any human birth, not just Jesus'. They are blind to the miracles all around them for no other reason than that they see the "weird repetitions"[26] every day. Naturally, they miss the Ultimate Miracle silently growing in the womb of Mary. What about you? What do you say?

Is anything impossible with God?

If you were waiting in a slow-moving line of sick and dying ones, every sound of "I can see! I can walk! I am alive!" drifting back from the front of the line would light a fire in you. This is how I take my joy from the miracles of Christ . . . like one standing in a long line that leads to him. My time will come.

It's that kind of world.

And I love knowing how this world's story ends. The glory of Christ returning is not some cheap writer's ploy that doesn't fit our real-life story. It's what all things have been moving toward from the beginning—the renewal of all things through and in him. It started when he rose to life. It will end with joy in Christ, for ever and ever and ever.

He's that kind of God.

"But I'm pro-choice"

That which is growing inside Mary's womb—what is it? Is it birth material or an unborn child? a fetus or a baby? a human zygote or a miracle from God? What do you call it?

What do you call it when the Holy Spirit comes upon a virgin named Mary and the power of the Most High overshadows her? when he takes her unfertilized egg, just barely visible to the human eye, and in the secret place begins to knit together the body of Christ?

What do you call it when undiminished deity is contained within a single cell?

Do you understand that he will not merely come *from* this? that he will not somehow emerge *out of* it? That holy embryo is he himself. And from that humble beginning, he will pass through every stage of human life and development, redeeming each one, healing each one.

The angel called him the Son of God.

That day was a time of grace.

(Please read Luke 1:26-38.)

King David, around 1000 B.C., concluded that he was "fearfully and wonderfully made."[27] Consider that all he had seen of himself was human skin, which almost magically sewed itself back up when it was cut. It snapped his head back and lifted his eyes to the sky. A loose translation of David's original Hebrew is, "Wow!" We've been able to look a lot closer at the human body than David. Guess what? The mystery only deepens. Exponentially.

Have you ever seen two human heart cells dropped at opposite ends of a petri dish—how they begin to beat together to some unseen Conductor? Have you seen brain cells reach out to one another with tiny arms, grasping one another in a human thought? Cut your skin and at the far end of your body, white blood cells will begin their baffling march, elongating their bodies to squeeze through tissue and spending their tiny bits of life smothering any invader they meet.

But we can look even closer than that. Have you ever looked down an electron microscope at tiny spinning machines, bits of energy circling other bits at mind-numbing speeds, that laugh at every known law of the universe?

One more question. Have you ever seen your own unborn baby through an ultrasound? Remember how your heart pounded and your love awoke. And I ask, is this how one feels about a chance collection of molecules?

No.

It is wonderful. It is fearful. And scientific descriptions don't change it one bit. Science is mere observation. The magic is not explained. You can never get behind the curtain and say, "Ah, I see how he does it."

It is a miracle.

And King David may have come up with the most telling word ever thought of to describe unborn life in the womb when he referred to it as "me." He once wrote to God, "You knit *me* together in my mother's womb. My frame was not hidden from you when I was made in the secret place."[28] I didn't come *from* a fertilized egg any more than I came from a teenager or a toddler. I *was* a boy, before that a baby, and before that an embryo. That embryo may not have been medically viable, but it was, in a word, *me.*

It all started, that is, I started with a single cell. Lewis Thomas wrote about the union of sperm and egg in the single cell—the start of every human story: "The mere existence of that cell should be one of the greatest astonishments of the earth. People ought to be walking around all day, all through their waking hours, calling to each other in endless wonderment, talking of nothing else except that cell."[29] It is life, and we have no right to destroy it.

If there were no Word of God to guide us on the question of abortion, we could go to science instead and ask three compelling questions about that growing tissue in the woman's womb.

Is it alive?

Is it human?

Is it a person distinct from its mother?

By any definition of life you choose, by the humanity written into the DNA, by the genetic code of the unborn child that is different from that of any cell of the woman's body, science itself must answer "yes, yes, and yes." These facts are not in dispute.

But we need to ask deeper questions than these. For these we have to leave the barren world of the materialist behind, leave behind the semantic games and the arguing about rights. We need to come back to the real world, the one made by God, to ask, What is life worth? Where does its value come from? In the Christian circle, we don't talk about "quality of life"—on a scale of pleasure or productivity—to measure life's value. Bill Gates and a Down's syndrome child, the product of rape and the product of love all balance equally on the scale. They are alive. Their values lie in what they are to God—not trash, not accident, not animal, but special creations and designs by God, who stared at the blank canvas forever before he began, who wrote every day in his thoughts before each of them came to be, who thinks of nothing else the way he thinks of them.

You and your conscience need only be shocked awake by tiny body parts in plastic bags. Have we lost our minds? Let the spell be broken! The real world is a raging battleground between real evil and real good, and these are its casualties. Have we heard Satan whispering to that woman who is pregnant and afraid, "End it, destroy it . . . and it will be well with you"? Have men stood long enough behind women in the appalling silence of Adam, who stood there in the garden . . . saying nothing?

This is hard talk, I know, but I'm not trying to hurt you. But if I work too hard at not offending you, I will offend God instead. So I must tell you what I heard happily thumping along when the fetal heart monitor was turned on—I heard life—and I must ask why you don't hear it too. Perhaps there's a reason. I know women who have aborted their children, destroying part of themselves along with their babies. For a long time they had locked themselves into the pro-choice position, barricaded behind the propaganda that only made sense because they wanted it to. From where they stood, the truth was just too awful to see. That is, until Life came in and they found out there was grace even for this.

There is grace because of one holy embryo that silently grew in Mary.

People ought to call to one another during all their waking hours in endless wonderment, talking of nothing except that cell—*Immanuel,* which means "God come to be here with us." The child grew up and the man not only wept at our death but died of it and came to life again. All this he did to be able to say to you: "Twice mine! Once because I made you. Twice because having lost you, I bought you with my own blood." No matter what you've done. No matter what you've done.

No matter what you've done.

And so to all the discussions about life in science labs and lecture halls, we add our three little words that tell what life really is, that speak eloquently of its true value. Life is a time of grace. That window of time between conception and death is our time for the Holy Spirit to come upon us and the power of the Most High to overshadow us, our time to receive that forever kind of life by faith in Jesus.

My friend who pastors in Ternopil, Ukraine, writes me that they keep coming, the little babies who have survived saline abortions. He baptizes them, letting water and the Word run over their scarred foreheads.

Where sin abounds, grace does even more.

She was alone, in no position to give her new baby boy the best he could have. She was already struggling as a single parent. She would give her baby to a loving, childless couple. She would make them a family. It was the hardest thing she would ever do.

It was a beautiful choice.

I was with her in the hospital room the last time she held him. I remember all the questions she had about my Christian faith. "How can a God of love . . . ?" "What about those people who never hear . . . ?" "Where was he when I needed him?" I remember all her challenges.

But then, stroking her baby's face, she looked up at me and asked, "Do you think God brought me this child to bring me to him? Because God knows what it's like to give a Son away, doesn't he?"

It is a time of grace.

"These stories about Jesus are myth, not history"

Caesar Augustus paces before the assembled bachelors of Rome, then explodes, "You are murdering our future!" In his view they aren't "fathering their descendants," so he enacts laws to give advantages to those who settle down and have babies. Later, to know if his laws are working, he begins a project he'll list as number 8 in his life's achievements.

He calls for a census of the entire Roman world.

Roman soldiers ride into a far-off town of Galilee where a young woman is "showing." One of them decrees that all must be counted in their town of family origin. Mary has to catch her breath. You see, there was one last detail that had puzzled her: She lived in Nazareth while the prophecy told of the Messiah born in far-off Bethlehem. Now Caesar himself plays his unsuspecting part and orders her to "the town of David." She caresses her belly.

"We're going to Bethlehem."

As I picture the emperor of Rome in his palace room, I'm imagining one of the thousands of places where sacred and secular histories intersect. Scrolls are piled all around, including one from Judea, a backward province in the land of the Jews. On it is written something very close to this: "Joseph ben-Jacob . . . carpenter; Mary bath-loakim . . . his wife; Yeshua . . . first-born son."

How shocked Caesar would be to know that no one says "Lo Saturnalia" anymore, only "Merry Christmas"; or that we measure calendar years not from the founding of glorious Rome but from the birth of that Jewish peasant child; or that that birth was the event dividing all history into a before and after—the time when God drew near.

(I am indebted to historian Paul Maier and his book *In the Fullness of Time* for the historic details in this section. And I invite you to read and compare also Luke 2:1-7.)

Call the eyewitness biographies of Christ's life myths and I'll ask you if you've ever actually read one—a myth, I mean. Trust me. They don't read like this:

"In the fifteenth year of the reign of Tiberius Caesar—when Pontius Pilate was governor of Judea, Herod tetrarch of Galilee, his brother Philip tetrarch of Iturea and Traconitis, and Lysanias tetrarch of Abilene—during the high priesthood of Annas and Caiaphas, the word of God came . . ."[30]

That last phrase shimmers like a myth does, yet it is embedded in the rock-solidness of history. The historian Luke names the names, provides the places, establishes the dates. He anchors his account into history with verifiable facts. In so doing, he invites the intense scrutiny of scholars, historians, and archaeologists, scrutiny that can be applied to no other faith or philosophy. Did you realize that?

Other world religions have precious little to investigate. To belong to Islam, for example, means to rely on the testimony of one man, Muhammad, and the words he claimed to have received. You must find him credible in spite of countless glaring errors. (For example, the Qur'an mistakenly reports that Christians include Mary as a member of the Trinity.) In contrast, what Paul Maier calls the "historical advantage"[31] of Christianity is staggering—the history-long story of salvation intersects secular history at literally thousands of points. Real places. Real people. Real events. Your scrutiny is welcomed. It's the price we pay for that single, costly word of Luke's:

"Certainty."

"Since I myself have carefully investigated everything from the beginning, it seemed good . . . to write an orderly account . . . so that you may know the certainty of the things you have been taught."[32] It is not myth. It is history. It is certainty.

In a particular place, at a particular time, to one particular peasant girl . . .

It happened.

In fact, Luke's investigation likely had him asking Mary herself about the things she had pondered since she was perhaps just 15 years old, releasing the mystery and surprise we find in Luke chapters 1 and 2. Have you read these chapters?

It occurs to me that the best defense I could make for the eyewitness reports of Jesus' life—for Matthew, Mark, Luke, and John—would be to convince you to actually read them. Discover the surprisingly honest and realistic accounts written in newspaperlike detail: the 12 baskets of leftovers when Jesus fed the five thousand, the exact amount of water that he changed into wine, even the irrelevant things Peter kept saying. C. S. Lewis pointed out that if these were fabricated stories, some rather ordinary men invented a genre of literature, "realistic historic fiction," that would not appear again for some 1,800 years.

The truth is in the details. The gospels carry that irresistible ring of authenticity that has been termed *verisimilitude*. For example, if you were fabricating stories about Jesus in an attempt to make something of him that he never was, why in the world would you have the last recorded words of his forerunner, John the Baptist, be, "Are you the one who was to come, or should we expect someone else?"[33] I can't think of a single reason. I can think of a hundred other examples.

We can understand the verses in which Jesus seems bound by human limitation, such as when he said he didn't know the date of his second coming or could do only a few miracles in Nazareth. We can work with Jesus' suggestion that the generation of people he was addressing would witness the coming of his kingdom. But we must realize that only authors who were committed to writing actual history would include such things. Clearly these witnesses did not feel at all free to omit troubling details.

If they had felt free to write what they wanted, would they have had the primary witnesses to Jesus' resurrection in that day and age be women? Would they have chosen a traitorous tax collector to write the gospel addressed to the Jewish audience? Would they have included the consistently embarrassing moments and almost constant misunderstandings of Jesus by the men they were trying to establish as the apostolic pillars in the emerging church? I can't imagine why. In *The Case for Christ,* Lee Strobel scrutinizes the eyewitness testimonies of the gospel writers according to eight standards commonly used in today's courts of law for testing the credibility of witnesses. The disciples pass with flying colors. The truth is, in the ancient apostles we find men who did not cover up information that was dreadfully embarrassing to them, men whose accounts were accepted as factual while thousands were alive who could have discredited them, witnesses whose testimonies were corroborated even by their enemies, and writers who had nothing to gain for lying but grisly deaths. Their character, as witnesses, is unimpeachable.

Even the apparent discrepancies between the four accounts are compelling internal evidence for their authenticity. The point is not merely that the problems can be solved, such as the seeming conflicting accounts of Easter Sunday. The beautiful thing to notice is the integrity of these witnesses. No attempt was made to get their stories straight or paper over the problems. Each wrote what he saw and heard and assembled a document according to his unique audience and purpose for writing. The resulting accounts are precisely what you would expect from honest witnesses. Besides, if the many witnesses of an automobile accident didn't seem, at first glance, to be in perfect agreement, would you conclude that no accident happened at all? Hardly. It's not as easy as that to dismiss the breathless wonder of Mary Magdalene.

"I have seen the Lord!"[34]

And the same arguments for integrity apply to all those in the early church who faithfully copied these accounts thousands of times over, seeming contradictions and inconvenient details and all. Call it all a pious hoax and you do not grasp the genius you are ascribing to those ordinary men, nor the magnitude of the conspiracy you are suggesting. Discredit the right of the New Testament documents to be taken at face value if you like, but first you'll need to toss out virtually all of ancient classical study and abandon every accepted standard of historic attestation. By those standards, if any ancient writing can ever be deemed historically reliable, it is the New Testament.

The truth is, as the documentary evidence continues to be sifted, more and more scholars of ancient church history are grudgingly accepting what the Sunday school child already knows. I refer to the flat-out stunning fact that the gospel of John was written . . . by John! (You see, some folks assumed this gospel, so clear about the deity of Christ, must have been written a couple centuries or more after his life . . . until the discovery of a fragment of John chapter 18 that had already made it to faraway Egypt by about A.D. 125.) This is only my latest, favorite example of a stubborn fact before which the prior assumptions of faithless scholars are made to bow.

"No one has ever seen God, but God the One and Only, who is at the Father's side, has made him known."[35]

Of course there are other so-called scholars who elevate any crumbling documents they can find that would seem to deface historic Christianity and place their "discoveries" on par with Matthew, Mark, Luke, and John. Never mind that their sources do read like myths or that they originate from several centuries later and from radical sects a hundred miles away. Never mind that without a scintilla of credible evidence they discredit the right of the gospels to be read at face value—out comes another book about the search for the real Jesus.

Biases and blind spots.

Vested interests and ulterior motives.

They don't want Christ to be Christ.

I like the observation of G. K. Chesterton: In a courtroom trial, when the matter is one of life and death, we listen to "experts" but never entirely trust the issue to them. Instead we gather 12 ordinary people to make the final verdict, just as our Lord Jesus himself once did. So listen to the ones who can say, "We were there." Hear Peter promising us all, "We did not follow cleverly invented stories when we told you about the power and coming of our Lord Jesus Christ, but we were eyewitnesses of his majesty."[36] Myth? Peter was writing about someone he knew. John chimed in as well, "That . . . which we have seen with our eyes, which we have looked at and our hands have touched—this we proclaim concerning the Word of life."[37]

With words like these I am drawn inside the glow of that apostolic circle. We are seeing something together. Standing beside the likes of Peter, James, and John, contemplating the real Jesus, the search is over. He found me. Their Spirit-inspired testimonies are my certainty.

I suppose I could now invite you to read all 742 pages of Josh McDowell's *The New Evidence That Demands a Verdict*. Among other things, you would be overwhelmed by all the archaeological data and all the ancient historical voices that line up in overwhelming support of the Christian faith. Although such studies serve a purpose, there is a curious air of irrelevance hanging about them. At least for me there is. You see, when you're already certain of something, truly certain, any evidence for becomes just as inconsequential as seeming evidence against.

So it is with my heavenly Father and the love of Christ his Son.

I'll admit that it's exciting to see history repeatedly verify the things in the Bible, such as the ancient census of Caesar Augustus. Yet, in a deeper, truer, more fundamental way . . . I already knew. How?

"The Word of God came."

When were Romulus and Remus, the legendary founders of ancient Rome, born? When Zeus' head split open. This is what is meant by myth—its characteristic feel is not so difficult to detect.

When did God enter human history by means of a human birth?

"While Quirinius was governor of Syria . . . she gave birth to her firstborn, a son. She wrapped him in cloths and placed him in a manger, because there was no room for them in the inn."[38]

This is what we mean by certainty.

Ever since sin began, human beings have let their minds run with a fascinating question. "If there is a god, what is he like?" Human answers come pouring in.

We've heard about God as an impersonal force, as unfeeling as a jolt of electricity. God as tolerant grandfather, wanting all to be happy in their own ways. God as a cosmic bookkeeper, who lives to catch us doing wrong. God with his hands full, a higher power who wishes he could do more to help. God as a crutch, which the weak dreamed up. God as myth, as irrelevant idea, as not-so-harmless fiction invented by those hungry to control.

Maybe there are many gods. Maybe everything you see is god. Maybe we are god. Maybe, in some crazy way, god is all of the above. Maybe no matter what each person calls him, it all refers to the same god.

It's all just talk.

Across all the centuries of human speculation about God, however, there is one moment that is utterly unique.

" . . . and she gave birth to her firstborn, a son."

I see his hand wrapped around Joseph's thumb . . . then reaching for an untouchable leper . . . clawing the ground of Gethsemane . . . then being cruelly nailed to the wood. I see a scarred hand lifted up in blessing.

And I know who God is.

C. S. Lewis called Jesus the ultimate "iconoclast," that is, the One who came to smash in pieces every false image of God, to destroy every human representation of the divine, to once and for all demolish every uneducated guess about deity. Picture man-made statues crashing and smashing onto a marble floor, tongues of fire licking through canvas paintings, shafts of light entering the long, dark sanctuary, sparkling in the shards of stained glass. And in the midst of all the rubble . . . stands love . . . stands Jesus.

God made known, real, alive, in flesh and blood.[39]

"The radiance of God's glory."

"The exact representation of [God's] being."[40]

"No one has ever seen God, but God the One and Only, who is at the Father's side, has made him known."

(Please read John 1:1-18.)

My congregation rented space on a college campus for worship. When I arrived to set up the chapel for worship, I found her sitting in the dark. "I hope you don't mind my being here," she said. "I don't believe in God."

I borrowed a disarming response from author Bill Hybels: "Why don't you tell me about the God you don't believe in. Maybe I don't believe in him either."

Sure enough. The God she rejected was one that sits on his hands, does nothing about the pain of the world, watches like one watching a game, invents arbitrary rules to keep people ashamed and afraid, and finds delight in passing his killing judgments. It was a pleasure to say to her: "Guess what? I don't believe in that God either. He doesn't exist."

"So what is your God like?"

I thought she'd never ask.

My God is the God of music and laughing, of science and beauty, of patient justice and tender mercy, of everything that is alive and everything that is good. He is not far from you if you think you know what love is or forgiveness or meaning or hope. My God is the inventor of fireflies and the one who first thought of the cool summer nights in which they could fly. My God is the one you may thank for your shoes and the feet that you put in them. He is the binder of broken hearts and the God of second chances. My God is . . .

You get the idea. Perhaps a more orderly approach to that question is to think of God's attributes as revealed in his own Word, the Bible. (By the way, I'll be doing this throughout this book. It's called honest authority referencing. I hope by the time we're done, you'll see that this makes more sense than believing the Ted Turners and Shirley MacLaines of the world just because they say so.) So . . . here goes.

God is omnipotent. He is able effortlessly to accomplish anything by the awesome power of his own will, including the creation of matter, energy, space, and time out of nothing and including the astounding creation of our world and all that is in it within a single unhurried week. Of course, certain challenges to God's power that you could name are self-contradictory: "Can he make a rock so big he can't lift it?" "Can he make a square circle?" C. S. Lewis commented once that nonsense doesn't stop being nonsense just because we're talking about God.

God is omniscient. He not only knows everything that could conceivably be known—the future and the past, the thoughts of every human being, the number of molecules in your body—but it is an effortless knowing. He does not need to pause and call such things to mind. He does not need a moment to count the hairs on your head. These things are ever before him. He just knows. He always sees to the essence of everything and to the very core of us.

God is omnipresent. This doesn't only mean that he fills the vastness of the universe with his presence. That could make you think that in the quiet corner where you sit reading, there is some tiny part of him. God is not divisible into parts. The mystery of the God who is all-present is that God in his entirety is found in every place. The universe is contained in him who is contained in the single seed. Blessed be his name.

God is eternal. This does not merely mean he has lived for a long, long time. As Creator of time itself, he exists outside of it. There is no succession of events with him. He has no yesterday and no tomorrow. He lives in an eternal present, without beginning or end. "A day is like a thousand years."[41] My birth, my life, my death, and my glory are all right now to him. As an author lives independently from the stream of time in his novel, God lives forever in a single moment of ours.

There are many more attributes. He is unchanging, just, and holy, despising, condemning, and inexorably opposing every evil and ungodly thing, including the evil in our own fallen human nature. He is infinite goodness. He is love. While our minds get a hold of these attributes of God by considering them separately, to sense their essential unity you may ponder them in any combination you choose. His omnipotence is omnipresent. His omniscience is eternal. His love is holy.

Then there are the related attributes of God, namely, that he is transcendent and ineffable. You see, God is "wholly other," utterly separate and set apart from every created thing. He exists in sublime independence, needing nothing whatsoever from us. "As the heavens are higher than the earth,"[42] so far beyond our finite human comprehension is God. While it's true, as Luther said, that all our talk of God is a "stammering and a stuttering," it doesn't mean there can be no talk. What it does mean is that for us to know God as he desires to be known—for he is personal—he needed to reveal himself. We just needed him to tell us about himself. His words, those we find in the Bible, are the ones that matter.

Ours don't.

The central message of the Scriptures is that God has revealed himself in Christ his Son, the "Word made flesh." The one thing God has been longing to say to his world . . . is Jesus. That's why, when someone sitting in the dark wants to know, "What is God like?"—does he laugh or cry or do anything at all?—my best answer is to draw him or her near to "God with skin on," that is, to Jesus Christ as the Bible faithfully portrays him. He is the perfect manifestation of God in human terms.

I answer by pointing to the One who held all the qualities of God hidden within the disguise of human skin, who knew "all that was going to happen to him"[43] one dark night of his own. I answer with the One who made the very beam of wood that got too heavy for him to carry up a death-shaped hill. There he would suffer inside the thunderclap, the meeting of God's infinite holiness and his infinite love—God's responsibility to judge and his mysterious impulse to save. I answer with the One who could do everything, hanging there doing nothing. Just dying. For me. I answer with love in flesh and blood, standing there alive again. "I am with you always, to the very end of the age."[44]

That's what my God is like.

All-powerful. All-knowing. All-present. All I need.

I love his attributes. I think of my cousin who died in a car crash. As that truck crossed the center line, knowing her as I did, I imagine her crying, "Jesus!" if only in her mind. I think of God who had forever to listen to that prayer. I unhinge my mind, strip God of human limitations, and know that though millions pray to him, I have his undivided attention as he draws near to interpret my sigh. I tremble that God should live in me by this beautiful faith. Not some piece of God. God. I look forward to seeing him with these two eyes, and death has nothing to say about it.

One day the questions I pose in this book will not merely be answered, they will dissolve in appropriate humility and awe. They will be overwhelmed by the goodness, the glory, and, above all, the perfect love. Once I have seen him with my own eyes, I'll realize that I was asking "things too wonderful for me to know."[45]

Blessed be his name.

Some think that they should be able to figure out God with their limited rational minds, and they end up in frustration. We in Christ find the mystery of God a holy pleasure to adore. We find humble fascination with God to be wonderful and liberating. It's the difference between straining to row a boat across a vast ocean and serenely drifting upon it.

The ocean in this analogy is God.

The wind is his Spirit.

We ride in awe and safety upon Christ, the Word of God.

"I believe what I can see"

God gave Simeon a promise: before his death, he would lay his eyes on the Messiah. One day, in some way, as those fading eyes scanned the faces in the temple courts like always, the fragrance of Christ met Simeon on a holy breeze.

Simeon saw *them*.

He shuffled over to two peasants and their tiny baby. He took little Yeshua in his arms. When Simeon spoke, it wasn't, "What a strong little guy," but "Sovereign Lord." His first words were not explanation to startled parents, but praise to the living God.

What Simeon said in that moment was that his life was complete, that death was his friend, that God kept his promise, that Simeon stared into the face of salvation and felt the warm light of glory on his face.

The wonder is that when Simeon said all this, he was looking at a baby.

This was Simeon's gift—to gaze at an infant and see far more.

The Spirit helped Simeon over the scriptural dilemma, the conflict between faith and sight. We're all asked to trust things we've never seen on the promise of Someone we've never met. The wait-and-see approach will not do. We would miss out on everything that means anything at all.

Some things have to be believed to be seen.
(Please read Luke 2:21-35.)

To a materialist, everything can be explained in a natura-
listic way, no matter how thick the cloud of mystery that
hangs about it. What you call being in love is a chemical
reaction in the brain that is built by a long, slow evolution.
Things happening just the right way are not providence but
coincidence. The assurance that God is gracious for Jesus'
sake is only my peculiar psychology and the way I've been
conditioned. It's all so simple; the truth is seen once you
break each thing down.

The term is *reductionism*. Every wonderful thing can be
reduced. Art comes down to blotches of color on a canvas.
Music is merely a combination of sound waves that strangely
pleases our minds. The worship making my spirit whole is
ultimately chemicals at play in my skull. The things you can
see and touch, vivisect and analyze, these are real. Meaning,
hope, morality, truth are mere thoughts in our heads, odd-
shaped crutches on which the mind keeps leaning.

My costly faith is mild neurosis. That's all.

Yet I notice that those who think this way still feel
something penetrating and deep—something very close to
gratitude—at their baby's first cry. They gaze up at the
same stars I do and the impossible spaces between. They
know pleasures and joys they have not begun to explain.
Still they say, "There is nothing more."

The apostle James took that other point of view: "Every
good and perfect gift is from above, coming down from the
Father of the heavenly lights."[46]

Try savoring a delicious aroma drifting from the kitchen
without your mind naming its source: "Ah . . . fresh-baked

bread." So much of the pleasure of the scent is your antic-
ipation of the thing itself. Similarly, every good thing in this
world is a whiff of heaven. Can you glimpse the outrageous color, the red-on-purple sunrise, and not think, "Ah
. . . God"? Can you truly enjoy a sunset when you have no
one to thank for it . . . or before you realize you don't
deserve it?

How can you not follow the gift's glowing trail back to
the Giver?

Given such artistic glory on a canvas so grand, those who
see only blotches hardly seem qualified to comment.

Hear them anyway. Although when writing his famous
essay, "Why I Am Not a Christian," Bertrand Russell seems
not to have bothered to crack open the New Testament, it
can be worthwhile listening to a humanist such as him speak
with evident integrity: "The center of me is always and eternally a terrible pain— a curious wild pain—a searching for
something beyond what the world contains."[47] The honesty
is admirable. The truth is, few atheists live and think consistently with their beliefs.

It would be too awful.

Take the ideas of meaning and hope. To be a consistent
atheist would mean abandoning any such ideas. For meaning to exist there must be "Someone to Mean it."[48] If in the
end the universe is cold and dead, it had no real purpose
from the start. And if life itself has no higher purpose, nothing within it does either. If atheism is true, we must abandon all hope and every worthwhile reason to live because
the death that waits at the end is the death of any motivation, save the satisfaction of animal desires.

Yet, meaning and hope are necessary to the mind,
thoughts not so easy to shake. The young man who stood
up in a debate claiming, "Nothing has meaning," clearly
thought his own sentence did . . . and gave himself away.
And we cannot survive without hope. Nothing kills the

human soul the way this one sentence does: "I have nothing to look forward to."

All this makes atheism an unworkable philosophy: though you don't believe in meaning and hope, you realize that survival depends on living as if you do.

What distinguished Frederick Nietzsche is that he was a consistent atheist. He mentally followed the godless path all the way to its inevitable conclusion: utter emptiness, unyielding despair, and societal collapse. See a gloomy man hunched over a desk in a dark, claustrophobic closet, quietly going insane—the man who came saying, "God is dead." Now step into the sun. Set that pathetic life side by side with the man of joy—the earth-shattering, ethically brilliant, self-sacrificing life of Christ. Someone said, "The glory of God is a man fully alive,"[49] and this is Jesus. Jesus came saying, "God Is," and lived in perfect harmony with that belief. In Nietzsche and Christ are two who lived consistently. But they cannot both be right.

I set before you death and life.

Atheism is not only unworkable, it's logically unjustifiable. A negative assertion—there is no God—cannot be proven. Sensing this, many people fall back to an agnostic position, assuming that ground is more defensible. What they say is, "I don't know whether there is a God or not." As this philosophy works its way into real life, it becomes clear what they mean: "Until God is proven beyond any shadow of doubt, until there are no more questions that can be thought of, I will live on the assumption that he doesn't exist."

I have to ask, how much sense does it make to have that be your default position? What if we were talking about even a one-in-a-hundred chance that your family was in grave danger? Would you work on the assumption that everything's fine?

To bet against God and wager your soul that after death you're nothing but six feet under is not only to forfeit meaning and jettison hope, but it is to take the most horrendous gamble imaginable and to risk no possible recovery if you're wrong. But why?

Do you have an intellectual problem with believing in things you haven't seen? A young man said that to apologist Josh McDowell. The apologist answered, "Well, would you at least consider Christianity's claims if I put some tangible evidence in front of you that the New Testament is the most reliable piece of literature of antiquity, that its historic claims are consistently verified, that its . . ."

"No."

This, my friends, is not an intellectual problem at all. The problem is not with the mind, but the will. If you aren't able even to listen to the possibility of Christ, in spite of everything I'm trying to teach you, I suggest it's because you do not want to. There is no other reason. God has not failed to provide compelling reasons to acknowledge him. The human will has motives all its own. For the sake of its own shabby self-interests, it routinely decides against God and his perfect self-expressions: his Word, his Son, and the Spirit he sends. Do you plan to evade the reality to which everything that is dependable points? . . . until it's proven before your eyes? . . . until it's too late? Does this make sense to you?

When the apostle Paul met people who shrugged their shoulders in worship of a question mark—they had erected an empty altar "TO AN UNKNOWN GOD"—he answered, "In the past God overlooked such ignorance . . . now he commands all people everywhere to repent."[50]

After all, what if Christ is true? What if God had to reduce himself to nothing but a helpless child? What if divinity had to appear in a dimmed and muted way so that we might, for once, be able to hear him and look straight at him and not be consumed? What if there's more to Christianity than sprinkled water and bits of ink on ancient paper? "I have summoned you by name; you are mine."[51] What if there is more than meets the eyes in the broken bread and sips of wine? "My body . . . my blood . . . for you," said Jesus.

What if the Man on the cross was not only a Man? What if the Scriptures are nothing less than the voice of the almighty God, meeting your soul, overcoming your resistance, crying, "Take this. This is for you"? Indeed, God wraps himself in these means of grace. The hidden God is revealed in the Word and the water, the bread and the wine . . . and, preeminently, in the crib of Bethlehem.

Blessed, truly blessed, "are those who have not seen and yet have believed."[52]

We sinners don't need to know what the invisible God looks like. We need to know his heart, his will, his verdict on us. For that, there have to be words. Our real need has always been for him to speak in a way that we can somehow bear to hear his words.

Thank God for God. He has spoken with a "still, small voice." He has said something to this world through his only Son that will never be unsaid. With Word and water, bread and wine, God comes all the way down to us, calling us "forgiven," calling us "his."

And we follow these piercing shafts of day back to the Father of the heavenly lights.

"What kind of God demands worship?"

Their star-chasing journey comes to a satisfying end. Wise men from the East get down on their knees, down to the level of a child, and pour out their treasure.

Gold.

Frankincense.

Myrrh.

This bending low, this surrender of treasure—these are the outward actions that display the reality within. At the feet of a little boy, they perform the worship that is a promise of things to come.

One day raging winds will instantly die away at the simple command of Christ. Something new will come alive in a boat full of disciples. Floating there on a smooth, glassy sea, they too will worship him.

When Jesus rides a donkey into Jerusalem, the melody of the children will italicize the words, "Hosanna! Lord, save us!" The grown-ups will be alarmed. "Jesus, they go too far. They say too much. Make them stop." He could, I suppose. But the very stones on the ground will be biting their lips, biding their time, waiting their turns.

The women will look so lost among the tombs, searching for Christ in the last place he ought to be. There he will be . . . alive! They will bend low to wrap themselves

around his feet, lost in the delight of worship—that holy
pleasure of feeling so wonderfully safe and small beside
one so great.

Faithful ones will keep their appointments on a sacred
mountain. Even when he disappears from their sights into
heaven—especially then—they will worship. On this side
the spontaneous motion of knees fully bending, on the
other side the shouts of glory welcoming him home.

What do all these scenes have in common?

In not one of them is anyone heard barking out the
order to praise. When these people worship, it's not
because anyone tells them to. No one needs to. They
adore Jesus . . . because they see him.

The gold is given outright.

The frankincense releases its lovely scent.

The myrrh pours out.

And here's the beauty of it: This worship is not so much
their gift to God . . .

It's his gift to them.

(Please read Matthew 2:1-12.)

God demands our praise.

For some it's a stumbling block: What kind of primitive
concept of God is this? Is the Lord like the vain man who
demands and depends on admiration? Is he like the needy
woman who fishes for compliments that are never enough?

No. He's nothing like that.

My God is the God of music and singing. We only balk
at his call to worship until we understand what worship is.

During my college years, I toured the imposing New
York Metropolitan Museum of Art planted on the corner of
Central Park. I used to take a perverse pride in the fact that

I had seen the whole thing in about two hours . . . as if the pieces of art were no big deal. I'm not so proud of that anymore, my fast walk through one of the finest art collections in the world. Now I think it means I was stupid, insensitive to beauty, the loser who walked away from such an opportunity with nothing!

I would like to go back. I'm imagining how it might be if someone very different from me, not so halfhearted, were taking me on a tour of a large art museum. We approach Van Gogh's *Starry Night,* let's say. While I stand there with a puzzled frown, ready to move on, my guide lets out a breathless gasp.

"What?" I ask.

"So much pain," he whispers, tears welling up.

Next, Manet's portrait of a woman with her daughter. I scratch my head, while my guide very nearly groans. "What now?" I ask.

"He loved her," he says in a hush, not pulling his eyes away.

He is praising the works and the artists who created them. He is spontaneously trying to share the praise, to invite me into the hush he occupies. He's asking me to join him in his appreciation, trying to wake me up to the moving experience he's having, wanting a little of that sigh, that groan to come out of me as well.

That's what you do when you're praising something, when you love something, when you're grateful to something for lifting you out of yourself. Your joy and delight aren't complete until you express it . . . and you do. It shows up unconsciously and unstoppably on your lips.

I'm going a long way around just to explain what worship is. There are certain things in this world that happen to deserve praise. There are certain things that are worthy of awe, things for which the only appropriate, healthy human response is to say "Wow." Not to say

"Wow" is to be the loser, the ridiculous one who walked away with nothing.

The plain truth is that God is the ultimate artist to admire and enjoy, and for these actions we were made. Complain that God wants us to praise him and you might as well complain that God wants to fulfill us, make our lives worthwhile, and fill us with the one thing that fits the peculiar, empty shape in our souls . . . himself. The appropriate human response to God's work is to fall on our faces in worship. The biblical prophets and psalmists don't praise the way they do—"Whom have I in heaven but you? And earth has nothing I desire besides you"[53]—because they're supposed to, of all things. They praise because they see. They worship because God has revealed something of himself. Not to praise is to lose the greatest experience, to miss out on life's purpose, and to forfeit the only thing that makes any sense. Indeed, God says through the prophet Isaiah that he is the one "creating praise on the lips of the mourners in Israel,"[54] for this heals them.

What is wrong with us, so coldly asking if we have to worship? To have no heart for the very thing for which we were made is to have been cut off from ourselves somehow. What we don't see in this self-obsessed culture is that worship holds everything self-esteem never could. This world's call toward fascination with ourselves is a shabby substitute. Our selfish preoccupation is making us miserable. If we don't worship God, it's because we don't see God. We don't see that he is our life. To fail to see is to miss out on everything that means anything. It is to lose and be lost, to have a grumble built into your point of view, and to be doomed to go on grumbling forever.

This doom is what we deserve.

Yet there was one who had a heart of praise, who was able to look back on an entire life and say, "[Father,] I have brought you glory on earth."[55] Jesus alone could survey the life he lived here and say, "Father, I caused praise to come to you in all things. What I was born to do, I have done." Even his death, in spite of the horrifying circumstances, was an act of final, serene devotion. Like precious wine poured out on a most holy altar, Jesus abandoned his soul to his heavenly Father: "Into your hands I commit my spirit."[56]

Yet, I don't portray Jesus' heart of praise to give you an example—you should be more like that. The truth is much deeper. He was living the life you were meant to live but couldn't. You and I, we have no righteousness of our own in the sight of God. But in page after page of the gospels, we see Jesus fashioning out of the countless, flawless moments of his own exquisite life that glorious "robe of righteousness" to cover us in the sight of our God by faith. When you die, it can be his life that flashes before your eyes, not your own. For, through faith in Jesus, it is Jesus' fragrant life that God will be looking at when he says to you, "Well done! Welcome home!"

A rock star wears a crucifix because, in her words, "It's sexy!" Go ahead. Let her words hurt your eyes. She sees the man on the cross.

So much pain.

So much love.

She comes away with less than nothing. Not so the Roman centurion. Something rose to his lips and has risen to millions of lips ever since. It follows fast on the sudden, sharp inhale:

"Surely he was the Son of God!"[57]

The first rustling of praise in me tells me that I have not walked away with nothing. This is the Spirit's deposit, guaranteeing that I'll be praising him forever in a heaven only Christians really want. We will spend forever trying to adequately describe our Savior. We misplaced adjectives will meet our proper Noun.

We are dull and dim if we wonder how much fun it will be just to worship forever. Imagine being perfectly in love with God. We will finally be able to admire perfectly, to adore and delight ecstatically in the one who is worthy. We will be drunk in, washed over, dissolved into, and carried away with the enjoyment of him. Shouting "Wow" to him. Singing "Glory!" And crying to those on our right and our left, "Look at him. Just look. Do you see him?"

Yes, they see him too.

"Glory has come to me through them."[58] This is Jesus talking to his Father about his disciples. If you know anything about them, right now you're wondering, "through them"!?

"Through them."

Though we still struggle with ourselves, crushed by what we find within, we can still look to God and say: "It is me he loves. I treated him as nothing at all, so he became as nothing to save me."

With my heartfelt thank you, my stammering praise, Jesus has brought glory to his Father through me. Yes, through me, and you too.

"There are

no moral

absolutes"

A baby wrapped in "swaddling clothes."

All heaven breaking loose over a sheep-scattered hill.

Well-weathered shepherds hoarsely whisper, "May we see him?"

Wise men on camels, silhouetted against a diamond sky.

Lovely. But there is a part of the Christmas story that doesn't make the Christmas cards: Joseph snaps his eyes open. He's had a bad dream. "Mary, get up! Get Jesus! We've got to get out of here! He wants to kill our son!"

"He" is King Herod, a man of legendary cruelty—the kind of man who plans a mass murder to take place at the moment of his death to make sure that someone, somewhere will be crying. On this occasion, he has heard rumors of the birth of a little rival king, born right under his nose. He follows the treasure map of prophecy to a hole in the wall called Bethlehem. There he gladly wipes out a couple dozen little boys in the gruesome hopes of killing this one.

So the Holy Family flees for their lives, leaving the sound of weeping behind them . . . for the time being.

The boys of Bethlehem—they were just little kids! Their moms refuse to be comforted in this scene that doesn't appear in many

Christmas pageants. Make no mistake, however, this account deserves prominence in the Christmas story. Because into such a world the Christ was born. For such a world.

By all means, take a good hard look at humankind when it lives away from God. Look closely at King Herod. There's nothing he would not do. Without the restraining morality and justice that depend on God, there's no good reason for people not to act out the ugliest impulses of their hearts. As Russian author Dostoyevsky said, "If God is dead, everything is justifiable."[59] Folks may even try to kill God if they want to.

It's been done before.

(Please read Matthew 2:1-18.)

Is there no unchanging moral lawgiver and so no fixed and ageless morality?

Someone has pointed out how difficult it is to argue with people who deny what everyone knows. That happens to be the etymology of the word *conscience*—that which we all "together know." Though you may question the existence of moral absolutes, I suggest to you that you already know better. You only have to get quiet and still to realize that your innate sense of good and evil, of right and wrong, of should and should not comes from the same One the sunsets and foxes do. How can you even suggest that God has not revealed himself to you? The nearest, most present voice of God whispering, "I AM," is the pain you feel when you've caused others pain and even the pleasure you feel when you've given them a smile. Everyone knows this.

The Bible itself makes this point about even those people who haven't given the Bible a second thought: "They show that the requirements of the law are written on their hearts, their consciences also bearing witness, and their thoughts now accusing, now even defending them."[60]

I can hear you objecting, "I don't need to believe in some God to lead a good and decent moral life." Please don't miss my point. I realize that you are a likable person doing the best you can. What I'm really asking in all this is just where your sense of morality comes from in the first place and whether you even know what you mean by "good"?

Can it really be that there is nothing objective behind something so universal and unshakable as our human sense of right and wrong? It's too dependable. The inner voice is far too loud—the one that shouts, "You should not have done that," when we have known better. There is a sense of moral good and bad that comes naturally to every human being in essentially the same form. This inner command, the one trying to get us to behave in certain ways, is no mere social convention. It transcends culture as clearly as 2 plus 2 equals 4 all around the world. Flawed though we are, God's own will regarding the sort of people we must be is deeply impressed upon our nature as a dim reflection of his. That will doesn't change, because God doesn't. It's a phenomenon that no anthropologist can sufficiently explain. An evolution driven by survival of the fittest can never explain this sense that people should not live just for themselves.

Or the guilty awareness that we do.

Here is a clue, as C. S. Lewis observed, to the meaning of the universe. We know both that we must answer to Someone for how we live and what we are . . . and that we can't. This explains the fact that, as someone has said, "Every society erects an altar."

An altar? I can hear you saying at this point, "Don't some people actually kill in the name of God? Didn't almost three thousand people perish in New York City at the hands of militant worshipers of Allah?" I freely admit, as a matter of doctrine, that the human conscience can be distorted and twisted almost beyond recognition. Journalist Malcolm Muggeridge commented that the most empirically verifiable part of the human experience is the depravity of human-kind.[61] (More on the doctrine of original sin another time.) And yes, consciences can be dulled. Perhaps lies and lust don't hurt you or me as much as they used to. The thing to notice right now is the way you cannot be talked out of your own sense of just how wrong certain things are—wrong for a bigger reason than the mere fact that you think so or that society currently does. In fact, anytime you so much as say the word "should" to anyone, you unconsciously appeal to some standard outside of you both that you expect that person to know and agree with. Your words give you away.

Think for one unpleasant moment about a child being abused or a woman being raped. I ask you, should this happen or should it not? And if not, why not? You might be shocked to discover, from a philosophical point of view, how elusive the reasons become. If you remove God from the picture, then ultimately right and wrong are only thoughts in our own heads. As is often pointed out, these thoughts would be mere preferences of ours—like preferring chocolate to vanilla. (Are we ready to admit that we lock criminals away for life on nothing more than our opinion about right and wrong?)

Tell me that we should live in this or that way for the good of society, and I'll ask why in the world, if atheism were true, I ought to care about that. Although you want to tell me I just should, perhaps you realize that you lack the vocabulary to explain why.

The best-informed atheists are those who shrug their shoulders and admit the inability of atheism to supply a compelling reason, if there is no God, to do good. Are such things as molestation and murder wrong for no other reason than that we say so? That means that if our preferences change and if we as a race cheerfully declare them "okay" tomorrow, they will be!

Does this sound right to you?

Is there not something unchanging in the universe that says in an unchangeable way, "This should not be"? Is there not Someone besides us who spells Right and Wrong in capital letters? The truth is, you really think those who do such things are actually wrong, not just that they have different preferences than you do.

You've always sensed, haven't you, how hollow are the sounds of ethical discussions that refuse to trace the persistent whisper of conscience back to its Source. It has come in vogue again to hear the word *evil* in the media, especially since the vicious attack on civilians at the World Trade Center in 2001. Probe the columnists, however, and you may find that they still think of evil as a social construction, the sort of thing cultures merely invent over time but that lacks any reality. One man, when pressed for his opinion, said that, yes, there is no real, objective difference between cruelty and non-cruelty. A second man held a kettle of boiling water over his head and asked him the question again.

How empty are society's plaintive words amid the anguish of these troubled times . . . until someone makes the one argument people so strangely keep resisting.

Why shouldn't such things as cruelty and terrorism be? Why is *evil* the right word for the things people do? Because God Is. That's why.

Perhaps the reason we so vehemently deny the Holy One is because the implications of his existence are too hard for the unholy to take. We are the ones who argue in favor of sexual immorality. We cling to our right to satisfy ourselves. We find gossip to be delicious, even as we destroy someone's name. We love what we know is wrong. We knew what innocence was and felt its loveliness . . . but could not help ourselves from trampling it to dust. We find that our hearts incline toward very bad things.

While honesty, love, and purity are so self-evidently good, we secretly realize that somehow, in the story of the universe, we're the bad guys. We don't know how that happened, only that it did. We think the answer is to deny what everybody knows.

Some time ago a modern parable appeared in the form of a jarring account in the newspaper. A 14-year-old boy killed his father. The police had him in custody and asked him why he did it. He said, "He was always after me, always telling me what to do. I couldn't stand him." The reporter wrote that on that very night, at the detention center where the boy was being held, a guard walking down the hallway heard the boy sobbing, "I want my father. . . . I want my father."[62]

In a society determined to make its own way, to cut itself loose and somehow to make life make sense apart from our Father, there is still the ache in the middle of the night. For if there were no absolute morality, then neither would there be absolute Love.

But there is. Into such a world the Christ was born. For such a world.

Morality does exist, because God does. I was meant to be like Jesus, knowing only worship, living only love. But there's more than just love and worship going on inside me. In a way I fall every hour of every day.

This is the real reason I write about morality, to suggest the one soft place where you may land.

A stable.

A feeding trough.

A pile of hay.

One lovely spot where we may together know grace.
"Today in the town of David a Savior has been born to
you; he is Christ the Lord."[63]

"I can't understand your three-in-one God"

The child grew into a man of wisdom and stature, grace and gentle strength.

The son of a carpenter, he worked with his hands until one day it was time. The tools of the trade were carefully laid on a shelf.

A place for everything. Everything in its place.

The apron was hung from a peg by the door, which he quietly closed behind him.

"God bless our comings and our goings . . ." any Hebrew whispered as he left home, whether on his way to the market or to the synagogue.

Or to save the world.

Jesus made his appearance among the masses that were crowding the banks of the Jordan; he asked for his turn at being baptized by John. The Baptizer was incredulous. He could only stare at the ground, at a pair of sandals he was unworthy to stoop down and untie.

"Me? Baptize you?" he stammered.

Jesus insisted, so John baptized him.

When God the Son came up from the beautiful waters, God the Holy Spirit flew like a dove through a tear in the fabric of the sky. And with the heavens so laid bare, God the Father thundered as if the words could no longer be held back:

"I love my Son."

Another prophecy found its inevitable fulfillment. The Father had said: "Here is my Servant, whom I have chosen. I will put my Spirit on him . . . to open eyes that are blind, to free captives from prison, to release from the dungeon those who sit in darkness."

In other words, "It is time." So said the one and only God, blessed be his name. So said the voice, the lamb, the dove. It was time.

(Please read Matthew 3:13-17.)

I knew I had people in my congregation who thought they had the triune God all figured out. Simple, right? "He's like an egg—shell, yoke, and white—three parts but just one thing." "No, he's like water—it can take the form of liquid, ice, or vapor—what's so hard about that?" I wanted to make sure they knew one thing. They did not have him figured out.

I held up a large sphere, which stood for God.

Point 1: There is only one God. His name is the Lord. Swishing my hand around the sphere, I explained that God is one, indivisible essence. There is no dividing God into parts. "Hear, O Israel: The Lord our God, the Lord is one."[64]

Point 2: Who is God the Father? Swishing my hand again to indicate the sphere in its entirety, I announced, "The Father is God." The Father is not one-third part of God. He is wholly, fully God. Who is God the Son? Same swishing motion. Same point. "In Christ all the fullness of the Deity lives."[65] Who is God the Holy Spirit? Same explanation. Lie to him, the Scriptures say, and you've lied to God[66] . . . who is not even a little bit like an egg.

Point 3: Father, Son, and Holy Spirit are not merely different forms that this one, indivisible God takes, as if one time he's the Father, another time the Spirit or the Son. The analogy of water taking different forms is—sorry about this—all wet. Though each is fully God, the members of this Trinity are revealed throughout the Scriptures as distinct persons who relate to one another. The Father sends his Spirit. The Spirit comes to rest upon the Son. The Son prays to the Father. They speak to one another, honor one another, love one another.

We have one, indivisible God who is revealed in three distinct persons, each one fully God. . . . And to the quizzical we-don't-get-it looks in my congregation, I cheerfully announced, "Now you're getting it."

This is not something we figure out like a riddle. There is no earthly thing we can set beside God for purposes of easy comparison. We hold God by faith in mystery and awe—Father, Son, and Holy Spirit loving one another, each permeating the others in a oneness so profound that it strains reason and resists analogy.

As does the love. "God is love,"[67] the apostle John wrote. And this remains true, even if we are not in the picture at all. God is love within himself, an unfathomable community, an eternally unbroken circle. You might as well try to hold the ocean in a teaspoon as try to grasp this ineffable triune God with your finite mind.

It is better just to fall to your knees.

Now there is one analogy I'll venture, if you promise to follow carefully. I'm not the first to use it. Imagine if we existed in only two physical dimensions, as if all we had ever experienced was our flatland of height and width and we knew nothing of depth. Now imagine that someone who existed in three dimensions tried to communicate to us a mysterious concept called a solid. Let's say he tried to describe a cube to us. "Six square sides" wouldn't make any sense. He could certainly draw a cube on our flat surface, just as you can draw one on paper, but we would only see the lines, the squares, and the angles. "Yes, we know all about those," we would say. But we would never perceive the cube, never see into it. When we say the person describing it is wrong . . . well . . . we're wrong.

The point is not that God is like a cube. The point is this: Someone who exists in places where our thinking cannot possibly follow, beyond our dimensions of space and time, will almost certainly say things about himself that do not make sense to us. There's nothing unreasonable about recognizing the limits of our reason, especially when it comes to God talking about God. When we try to understand, the only thing that makes any sense is to say to our offended logic, "Shhhhhhh, the Lord is speaking."

How many times in the course of scientific investigation have our best minds assumed that the truth, once we find it, is something very simple and predictable? Instead of the tiny, unbreakable balls that our best and brightest thought would be at the bottom of all matter, we met wild, whirling universes, inconceivably small. So why can't there be a wild, unpredictable Someone beneath even those?

There is, after all, some phenomenal evidence that the Trinity is true.

First, bring together any three philosophers, even those from a single time and place, throw out any topic, and listen to them argue. Next, imagine all the ways it would be so easy to misspeak on the topic of the Trinity, as illusive to our understanding as it is, yet so clearly defined. Now, consider the 40 or so authors of the Bible spread across 15 centuries writing about God's triune nature with perfect consistency, with remarkable and demonstrable harmony. Perceive the miracle of biblical revelation.

God peeled back the veil while Isaiah stood staring at six-winged angels. With two wings they flew. With two they covered their faces. With two they covered their feet. They cried out to one another until every shakable thing was shaken. What they cried in the presence of the Lord, blessed be his name, was not, "Sort of like water!" or "A little like an egg!" but, "Holy! Holy! Holy!"[68]

The triune God inhabiting the Scriptures was not revealed to frustrate our thinking but to let us see what he was willing to do for us. Juxtaposed against humanity's efforts to find God stands God's effort to find us. Compelling our truest worship is the fact that such a one would come for us in such a way—that on a miserable hill outside Jerusalem, nailed to a tree, the Son of God should cry, "My God, my God, why have you forsaken me?"[69] So complete was the identification of Jesus Christ with this whole world that "God made him . . . to be sin for us."[70] The guilt of us all was taken up into the Trinity itself, there to be atoned. Sin's awful power to separate—you've felt that power in human relationships all your life—was felt between the Father and the Son as the Father turned his face away and the Son sank into hell. All Jesus had ever heard from his Father from all eternity was, "This is my Son, whom I love."[71] But on that one day, the eternally unbroken circle was broken.

To let you in.

Jesus prayed the night before it all happened: "Father, let the world know that you have loved them even as you have loved me. . . . May [they] be one, Father, just as you are in me and I am in you. . . . We are one: I in them and you in me."[72]

To paraphrase: "They're separated souls, Father, let's take them in, let's make them alive, whatever the cost. Let's let them have everything you and I have had for all eternity."

A place for everyone.
Everyone in his or her place.

And so the very skies opened up, as it were, on the day of my baptism. I was called a beloved son when the water came and the words were spoken:

"I baptize you in the name of the Father and of the Son and of the Holy Spirit."

The talk was flying over his head. Nicodemus struggled to keep up: "Jesus, I don't understand." With that, Nicodemus became the first ever to hear the sentence.

Does not this one sentence rise to the surface on the sea of human talk? Are these not the most important words ever spoken? And what is our part but merely the thoughtful spiritual inhale?

"For God . . ."

Pause. You can't picture the infinite Lord in your mind. We're too small for that. So conceive of him, as best you can, by his awesome works. Search his fingerprints. Let images play in front of you—your best sunset across your favorite lake, your sweetest memory of a moment you didn't create, your little girl. Do you remember God?

". . . so loved . . ."

Think of love. Have you ever felt a burst of love, almost unbearably sweet, as you looked down on your small, sleeping child? She seems to contribute nothing to the family but her demanding tantrums and her piercing midnight cries. All she offers is her own need. It is enough. She is everything. If you lost her, what would you give to feel her arms around your neck again? This love, the love of God, is the only why we can ever discern regarding the mystery that follows.

". . . the world . . ."

Think of the world, but don't just think of purple skies and mountain grandeur. Think of people, billions of people, and not only the nice ones. Think of looting mobs and seamy nightclubs. Imagine Auschwitz. Conjure up a crowd milling around a cross. They're laughing. This too is the world.

". . . that he gave . . ."

What does it mean just to give? No conditions. No strings. Unearned. Undeserved. One moment the thing is rightfully his, the next it is completely yours. A treasure is placed into empty hands. "I want you to have this."

". . . his one and only Son . . ."

Now think of Jesus. Think of him giving the little girl back to her mom and dad . . . and his pleasure so deep. Think of his ache to present Jerusalem back to his Father . . . as he cried so hard. Think of the one who would do anything for the feel of arms wrapped around him.

". . . that whoever believes in him . . ."

The word *believes* may jump out here, but I also want you to notice the next two words, *in him.* The reason is simple. Can the drowning man hang on to any old thing if he just hangs on hard enough? Can just anything be placed in the mouth of a starving woman? Will any old grown-up leg do for clinging to if you're a child lost in the mall? Can you really just believe "whatever you want, as long as you're sincere"? No. This particular sentence promises that whoever believes *in him . . .*

". . . shall not perish but have eternal life."

If these aren't the most important words in the world, it's because there are other words that hold the very same miracle. "Take heart, son; your sins are forgiven."[73]

"By grace you have been saved, though faith . . ."[74]

"It is finished."[75]

(Please read John 3:14-21.)

Word has gotten out among casual observers that we Christians believe "faith saves." Other people are chiming in that they believe their things as firmly as we believe ours, so what's the difference?

"Can't I believe whatever I want, as long as I'm sincere?"

I have to admit I'm a little puzzled by both halves of the question. When it comes to faith, believing "whatever I want" seems to be the one thing I cannot do. If I say I've deposited a million dollars in your bank account, you might believe me, but you more likely will not. Whether you want to believe has little to do with it. People can pretend about a lot of things, but we don't choose what, in our heart of hearts, we really believe, truly count on, actually trust.

To the second part of the question. The emphasis on sincerity makes me think you are using words like *believe* and *faith* differently than my Bible does. When you think any faith held sincerely enough ought to win God's approval, you're probably thinking of faith as some heroic human virtue. You might be thinking of the act of believing as the ultimate good thing we people can do to show God we're worthwhile after all. However, biblical faith is empty of any of that stuff we call merit. It has no earning power at all before God. It's not that kind of thing. To see it clearly, think about the grasping of a drowning man, the act of eating by a starving woman, the clinging of a child to a parent's leg—faith is only as good as what you have faith in. Since faith is merely a grasping, an apprehending, a clinging, everything depends on what faith is grasping, apprehending, or clinging.

Sincerity is an issue—pretended faith is no faith at all. My point is that *what* we are holding onto with our faith clearly comes first. Only after that is settled does the matter of how firmly we do this holding even enter the picture. This is an axiom in the pleasant circles in which I run:

"Faith does not save because of itself, but because of Christ, to whom it clings."

Here's how it works: The death of God's Son completely atoned for the entire human race. The accomplished fact was confirmed by his own cry from the cross when the suffering was enough: "It is finished." Nothing was left out. His resurrection on the third day proves it—everything depends on the certain Sunday morning when the world woke up redeemed, saved by God in Christ. "I forgive you" are the words now spoken by God to every human being. These words of good news are a promise from God that he indeed has done it all for us. The promise has been turned loose in the world . . . which brings me to the next axiom: "Faith requires a promise." You don't just believe, period. You don't merely believe whatever. You believe God when he says that he has reconciled you to himself through Christ, his Son. Saving faith is when God's message reaches your ears and, by the Holy Spirit, who has broken through your hard, yet crumbling, defenses, your heart says, "How blessed am I!"

That is, you trust him.

Faith does not complete the work of salvation nor add any bit of merit. It simply receives what God has done entirely without your help. In fact, notice that you are not being asked to believe something—that God loves you in Christ—that isn't really true until after you believe. His love for you is fact, whether you believe it yet or not. Whoever you are, you are part of that "world" that "God so loved." Those who forfeit this very salvation, their salvation, by refusing to believe will never be able to say that the gift wasn't given to them. It was. They wouldn't accept it.

When you understand precisely what was done on that hill outside Jerusalem, you know the words "you are forgiven" can truly be said to any human being. You even realize that the word *faith* doesn't necessarily need to be spoken to people for it to become their firm possession. Their eyes point to a cross. They hear that it is theirs. In some dark moment, or in many, they have seen their need. Now they smile a smile they've never known before.

I watch Abigail—"her father's joy"—sleeping. I feel a burst of love and want to compare it to the love of God. But it is a presumption. The truth is that, even in a moment like this, I have only dipped my toe into that great rolling ocean that is he. What love is this that gives an innocent Son for a guilty world? Do you see the truth and beauty of Christ? Do you want to have this gift? Then I tell you that, even if in a weak way, you already do. Christ crucified is pure foolishness to the natural self, but not to you . . . not anymore. Only understand that this emerging faith is not your gift to God. It is his gift to you. In the words of Christ, "You have not chosen me; I have chosen you." What matters now is that you keep your eyes on him, not on yourself and your level of sincerity.

Luther called it the "monster of uncertainty" to direct the poor sinner, desperate for assurance of peace with God, anywhere but to Christ crucified. There is a time not to think about how well or poorly we have served, how much we have been changed, how we think we feel inside, or even our own faith.

We don't have faith in faith. We don't hang on to hanging on.

We look away from ourselves to Jesus. Always. By a power not our own, we find ourselves gripping his promise: "Be of good cheer. I have taken your sin away."

We take it in our two hands. We hold it. We rest ourselves there.

Only there.

Faith, at its beautiful best, has a certain unconscious quality. Its eyes are not on itself but on that which it has grasped.

Think of a father who shows his little girl every single day how much he loves her. When she holds his hand as they walk along, she doesn't say, "Look at me, everybody. I'm really holding on now."

She's not *thinking* about the holding of his hand at all. She just does.

Go and study world religions. Read the best authors of our day who chime in on life's ultimate questions. While you're at it, ask the man on the street his ideas about relationships with God. One thing will become clear.

The following story is one only Jesus could have told.

Two men go to church. One stands up tall and vents all the pride in his heart. "I thank you, God, that I am not like other people." Then follows the dreary spiritual résumé, the detailed listing of all the good he's done. It's not a pretty sight, and yet he's merely saying what nearly everyone thinks.

"I work hard. I try my best. I don't do anything too seriously bad. I can think of worse people. I don't see any reason God shouldn't accept me. Isn't that what religion is about? Yes, do enough good, and God will accept you."

But in the back of the church sits a different man with a different spirit. He accepts the rebuke of the arrogant. It's true what people think of him. He only looks at himself and wonders how he got so far away. His fists tighten at his chest. He can't bear even to lift his face toward God. He makes no claim. There's nothing left to say but, "God, have mercy on a poor sinner."

The ending of Jesus' story is more radical than words can say. The rule writer up front was wrong. Dead wrong. He didn't get through to God. The man in the back did, and God lifted his awful burden. God called him innocent and sent him home with that lightness of step that only a few ever really know—only those who crawl safely into Christ by faith.
Washed clean.
No past.
A man five minutes old.
(Please read Luke 18:9-14.)

A wild and exciting movement has been set loose in the world. Please be a part of it. In nearly every place and all across history you can find them, those radical people who fell away from the "religion of works." Millions have cheerfully stepped off the treadmill on which they were endlessly driven to prove their worth. It was never enough. Then came Jesus, saying, "Enough, already. You're so tired. Come away from there."

"Come to me all you who are tired and weary, and I will give you rest."

At the foundation of every other religion you'll find that old compulsion—the deadly serious business of people wanting to save themselves. It might be the Hindu notion of Dharma or Buddha's Eightfold Path, the Five Pillars of Islam or the Ten Commandments. It might be the quasi-Christian idea of accepting Christ primarily as a moral example. I don't despise the people who embrace those religions. But they're breaking my heart. It's no way to live. The torturing idea seems hardwired into the human soul.

We think that the secret to life and to God's heart lies in our doing, well, something.

People will feel especially compelled to perform if the same thing was scrawled across their childhoods—if they found that acceptance had certain strings attached. Was parental love the carrot on the stick that was dangled always out of reach as your incentive to better behavior? "Be a good little boy or girl and then Mom and Dad will love you." But their reward was never given to the measure you longed for it. If it became your religion—"I'll earn love. Somehow, I'll deserve God."—you're not alone.

While virtually all religions have risen from that common soil, there is one religion set apart. Before you dismiss Jesus, the friend of sinners, realize just how different the Christian faith is.

First, Christianity is unique in its view of God's law. The standards set by God—"Love God with all your heart." "Love your neighbor as yourself."—are beautiful expressions of his holy character. We simply cannot live up to them. People assume the Ten Commandments were revealed to us so that we could enjoy God by obeying them. According to the Bible itself, nothing could be further from the truth.

"Through the law we become conscious of sin."[76]

The primary purpose of God's law is to show us our sins and our desperate need for mercy. The law is a bright and awful light under which we all wither, a dreadfully unflattering mirror before which we all stand naked. The reason God told us how we are supposed to live is so that we would understand, in no uncertain terms, that we fall short of what God righteously demands of us, that we are nothing like what we are supposed to be, that God is right to condemn us, that we have a problem and we ourselves are in no way the solution.

We must open our eyes to the yawning gulf between ourselves and God.

This is the very reason Jesus "spiritualized" the law. He taught that real conformity to God's will is a matter of the heart, not a matter of mere outward behavior. The one who lusts must plead guilty of adultery. The one who hates is a murderer. Such sins are not distinguishable to him who sees our hearts as plainly and effortlessly as he sees our actions. Thus Jesus raised the bar of performance so high that seeing it leads us to give up entirely. We throw our hands up, wondering, "Well, then, who could possibly have peace with God?" Indeed.

God brings us to this desperation because he loves us. The grace we need so urgently only sounds like good news to people who realize they are bad. It is a music that only those who despair of themselves can ever truly hear. These are the words:

"Through [Jesus] everyone who believes is justified from everything you could not be justified from by the law of Moses."[77]

To be justified means to receive a not guilty verdict from God, as from a judge in a courtroom. God stamps "Innocent" across our very lives for Jesus' sake through no merit of our own. His love is no carrot on a string. Salvation is unconditional because it is a finished fact for all human beings, no matter who they are. Forgiveness is freely given. Peace is laid into every lap. We, as beggars, hear someone all but begging us to take what he gives.

"We implore you on Christ's behalf: Be reconciled to God."[78]

Let my God replace a thousand condemning rules with a single, sweet command from Christ: "Do not be afraid." Trust not in yourself. Cling by simple trust to Christ, your substitute, to Jesus, your advocate in the presence of God. Believe in him who rose from the dead, and wrap your empty hands around the only salvation. Jesus is the way to God. There is no other. In him is the peace that doesn't depend on getting even a single thing done. Instead, you can smile and finally rest in him.

There is still more to the uniqueness of Christianity. I've known many religious people in my time, from Muslims to Jehovah's Witnesses, and from both my experience and my study, I have to say that there's a spirit in a Christian church that isn't found in a mosque or kingdom hall, a temple or tabernacle. I've never met a person outside of Christ who knew anything about serving God out of the pure desire to do so.

We don't have to serve God. We want to.

It's an utterly foreign thought that the others simply don't know how to think, no matter how "religious" they are.

You who follow other gods may slavishly strive to measure up if you must. Just don't call all that forced obedience *love*. That word is excluded. You cannot call the things you do for fear of being condemned love. Do not think you move God's heart as you attempt to buy his approval. Tell yourself what you like about your drivenness to "do good so God will accept you." Those works are dead to him.

Though I "surrender my body to the flames" or "give all I possess to the poor,"[79] my love for God hasn't even begun until I have found out how free, how willing, how costly, how complete is the way he loved me first. Only when I am secure in his grace and forgiveness does the possibility even exist that I can at long last begin to respond to my God freely, willingly, without guilt, without fear.

This is the thing only Christians know anything about. We heard the words of Jesus on the night before his death: "Where I go you cannot follow." He set us down in a quiet, safe spot, went over to that hill, and offered his body to a first-century crucifixion. We still sit breathless. We continue to watch.

And we love God.

After all, sinners living happily ever after because God was willing to die—this is the story only Jesus could have told.

"We love because he first loved us." This is a great truth. God's love always has been and always will be the first love. It's written largely across every aspect of the Christian life. Open the Word because you want to know him. Call out his name now though you never have before. Discover that he's been waiting all this time, that it is he who gently drew you.

Have you ever loved God? Do you love him now?

He loved you first.

"Marrying doesn't make sense anymore"

They asked Jesus, "Can a man divorce his wife for any reason?"

It was meant to be a hard question, but it wasn't difficult for Jesus to answer. For the answer Jesus only had to think back to the first Adam seeing the first Eve and to the delight in Adam's eyes when he noticed he wasn't alone anymore.

"Bone of my bones and flesh of my flesh,"[80] Adam cried when he could breathe.

So deeply had the Creator given them to each other that the two became "one flesh." "While I live, you'll never be alone," is the soul of marriage, the holy covenant given by God to people best not left alone.

So, on the question of divorce, Jesus answered, "What God has joined together, let man not separate."

"But . . . didn't Moses let a man just hand a certificate of divorce to his wife to be done with her? Isn't divorce just a piece of paper?"

". . . Because your hearts were hard," replied Christ.

Indeed, the only order Moses could bring to the chaos—all those people leaving all those people— was to get it all down on paper. "I divorce you, I divorce you, I divorce you," a man said and signed his name, and with that a living thing was severed in two.

The very "flesh of his flesh" was cut adrift.

It takes a Christian to see the horror of it.

You see, there's more still to marriage. The stubborn, unbroken, till-death-do-us-part commitment between a man and woman is a living, breathing portrait of the bond between Christ and his beaming bride, the Christian church. So beautiful, it's no wonder we cry at weddings. If marriage, even mine, manages to be a picture of that . . . what is divorce a picture of?

(Please read Matthew 19:1-9.)

Recently I met a man I instantly liked. Soon he was opening up to me about his divorce and about the woman he now lives with. He is in no hurry to marry her, because he "wants to do everything right this time." His heart doesn't strike me as hard, and there was not any irony in his voice. This is how far our culture has come. My new friend doesn't know what marriage is. But he does know a good deal more than I do about pain—the ripping of the sacred bond that he was once brave enough to make and the emotional blood that pools on the floor.

What about you? Are you looking for one good reason to keep your marriage vows now that love is gone . . . or to ever make such a promise in the first place? Marriage has been called an unconditional commitment to an imperfect person, which names both the beauty and the difficulty. In growing numbers, those both inside and outside of the covenant are asking, Is it worth it?

I ask a different question: How are you so sure that we can do without this thing called marriage?

Let's say you're a surgeon and you intend to operate on me to remove some internal part of me. I would first like to know that you know what this part does and what it's for. If you're not absolutely sure, may I suggest you leave it in place? My point is that I would feel a bit better about all those people cutting marriage out of our society little by little if I had some sense that they understood what it's for in the first place.

What is the purpose of all these weddings, of all the families you have watched being created as you sat before altar after altar? Have you given enough thought to the service that marriage has been performing for us for millennia and why it was lifted up in the first place?

"I do" is the stirring sound of the laying of society's foundation. It's the promise of parents who stay together, so that each child has one bedroom, not two in separate houses, and Mom and Dad's is down the hall. It's the promise of children growing up secure, marinated in the love between their father and mother, receiving from each parent what is uniquely his or hers to give. And it is knowing that when they become adults and it's their turn to create a family, they won't be inventing something they've never seen. The marriage vow is the promise of a new territory that husband and wife can find on the other side of all the things they've had to endure because they endured them together. I've seen people die in the presence of families that held together, with the "I love yous" flowing all around, and I've seen people die alone. I know which I would choose.

I've seen what this thing called marriage is for.

Not long ago I watched my mom care for my dad during his stay at a nursing home to recover from a stroke. She was still saying "good night" to him as I stepped out of the room. "It was a good day," she whispered to him about the ten hours she sat still in that overheated room. Her hand then slipped down over his heart. My parents are good together. It is good that my dad is not alone . . . it is good more than I can say. The love my mom shows him is like God in a way—though you may have never seen it, you cannot tell me there's no such thing.

Evidence that marriage makes sense comes in the form of statistics that say that "shacking up" is not a smart way to slide into marriages that will last. Confirmation is coming in from all sides in the form of the psychological, emotional, and even material devastation left in the wake of divorce, especially the devastation felt by the children.

Yet I come back to Jesus' answer. He made the one argument that is not allowed in our perverse culture anymore. Jesus brought up the covenant's Creator, the one who made male and female, the One who fashioned a single living unit out of Adam and Eve.

Why live this way and not another?

Because He Is.

"Keep the marriage bed pure" is a good law, given by a good God, who intends to provide for our best hope of long-term happiness in this otherwise lonely world. Stealing marriage's holy pleasures—and that's not an oxymoron—and ripping our sexuality out of its context of two people promised outright to each other degrades it. Calling divorce both a sin and thing God "hates" is, in the words of Chesterton, "the compliment God pays to the average man, taking him at his word."[81] And divorce as such, as a sin against God, is a bigger problem than all of society's emotional baggage combined.

The fact is that there is nothing that shows us our true colors quite the way marriage does. Nothing confronts us with the soul-searching question, Do I even know what love is? more than the way we've seen ourselves in the company of our spouses and have seen the rampant selfishness that one way or another makes marriages die on the vine.

My new friend, you want to do everything right this time? Confess whatever was wrong before. See the truth that your own past is trying to show you, as we all must. Recall the uglier moments of your life. Be sorry.

To know God at all is to know that ignoring or shutting him out is never the way. I don't just want you to "do everything right this time." I want you to know what love is, what grace is. This will make all the difference. Take a closer look at Jesus. Watch Love do what Love does. Jesus didn't insist on being free. He bound himself. He committed himself. He tied heavy burdens, our sin, on his own back for our sakes. He kept the breathtakingly brave promise he made before time began . . . to come for us. Our every failure to love killed him on that cross. If these words of your forgiveness are breaking through to you at all, you know what love is.

If you should decide to marry her, I want it to be because of a new and holy desire stirring inside you to love someone well, to go all the way, to give everything. It comes to you by the Word of Christ. Build it into your life together and nothing will be the same as it was last time. That is my promise to you, which my God will surely keep. In fact, in the daily living and forgiving that comes from him, you get to live out a picture of the greatest love story every told.

"As a bridegroom rejoices over his bride, so will your God rejoice over you."[82]

From what we know about first-century weddings, we can make a fair attempt at reconstructing a first-century marriage proposal. What might it have sounded like when a young man asked for a woman's hand, so that they could be bonded and inseparable for as long as he lived? What might he have said when he knelt beside her, offering his everything, promising that everything he was and everything he had would also be hers? It might go something like this:

"In my Father's house are many rooms; if it were not so, I would have told you. I am going there to prepare a place for you. And if I go and prepare a place for you, I will come back and take you to be with me that you also may be where I am."[83]

A man in a boat lost on the sea screams a tiny scream up to the empty sky, "Sir, I exist!"

The universe replies, "To me that is a matter of complete indifference."

Nature is *not* our mother. If anything, she is our temperamental sister; she comes from the same Parent we do, and she fell in the same Fall. With her killer whales and scorpions, she is as out of control as human nature is with its submerged anger and paralyzing fears. Her groans are as loud as a hurricane and as silent as a creeping virus. And, no, she doesn't happen to care about us.

Tornadoes can't be pleaded with.

Cancer has no compassion.

To them we are matters of complete indifference.

It's not the universe that answers our plaintive cry with, "I remember you . . . and I'm coming." It's Jesus, walking out on the waves to a boat battered by the wind.

The disciples cry, "It's a ghost," terrified at a distant figure in the dead of the night that seems to be suspended on the surface of the water.

"It is I. Don't be afraid."

"If it's you . . . tell me to come to you on the water." Peter says, just being Peter.

"Come."

As Peter gets out of his boat, we see to the heart of the matter of faith versus skepticism. This is not two world-views colliding—not the clash between religious faith and religious skepticism. This is between Jesus and Peter. It's one person calling to another.

"You can trust me."

Peter does. But then, when he takes another good, hard look at the water that can't possibly hold him and listens to the argument the wind is making and sees the mounding wave . . . "Ahhhhhhh!"

He begins to slip beneath the water. It is here that we get to see just what God does with the one who believes and also doubts. What does Jesus do about the miserable half-believer sinking down before him? "Jesus reached out his hand . . ."

"And caught him!"

When there is not enough faith to walk on water, there may still be just enough left to look up and cry, "Lord, save me." . . . And that is enough.

(Please read Matthew 14:22-33.)

Faith in Jesus Christ is not like believing that there's such a place as Tallahassee or that there once was a man named Napoleon. It's more than just accepting certain facts on good authority and sound evidence. Frederick Buechner once commented that believing that your house is on fire or that someone loves you might get you a little closer to what faith in Jesus is like—more than just your intellect is involved.[84]

Yet, do consider for a moment the way you believe that Tallahassee exists or Napoleon lived. Consider how limited your actual experience of the world is and how many facts like these you accept as fact though you've never seen, touched, or smelled them. In one way or another you are trusting the many someones who told you these things. And you are not unreasonable in doing so. You are right to believe them. Yet, make no mistake. . . .

You have not seen. But you believe.

What is unreasonable is to keep demanding absolute proof for everything you're asked to believe. That's not the way life is. You'll ruin every chicken sandwich by asking, Will this make me sick? and every ride home from work by obsessing, Will this kill me? and every "I love you" by demanding, "Prove it." In real life you eat the sandwich and start the car and receive the love because you are able to know that each is safe beyond any reasonable doubt . . . and that questioning everything would be paralyzing. It's no way to live.

Turning to the Christian faith, you can keep raising endless questions *ad nauseum,* refusing to believe until the proof is absolute. However, the problem will not be that God has failed to provide compelling reasons to believe in him. There are more than enough reasons to cast the verdict beyond all reasonable doubt that God Is and to live with it.

Remember that we are talking about your relationship with God, not a judgment about an ideology. The central question does have to do with an "I love you" coming your way. Your demand for absolute proof is asking for far less than God wants to give you, namely the intimacy of Christ's own Spirit working within you a relationship characterized by trust in the blood-dipped promises. That's a beautiful thing, believe me, and the kind of proof you're asking for would leave no room for it.

Oh, you'll have your proof one day. But what will it mean to bend your knees to Jesus . . . when to remain standing is no longer possible? It will be too late.

Instead, consider what G. K. Chesterton had to say about religious skepticism. God did not mean to stop all

questions dead in their tracks. God and his Word can stand
up to our honest questions. Go ahead and keep on doubt-
ing. Doubt this and doubt that . . . until one day you finally
"go all the way and doubt yourself."

May you come to have serious doubts . . . about your
doubts. Your mind that questions everything that comes
from God—that refuses to relax itself in the utter goodness
of him—could stand to be questioned. Just how reliable is
your skepticism? I must confess that the doubts arising from
my sinful nature are miserably self-serving. Acting like I'm
not sure would keep me from giving too much, saying too
much, or going too far in my self-sacrificing devotion to
God. While I'm quick to offer assurance that genuine, saving
faith exists in any Christian side by side with the incredulity
of our "flesh," I cannot at all consider that an innocent,
healthy skepticism. It's as bad as anything that is still wrong
with me. It is terrible that God speaks in his Word and something in me answers, "I'm not so sure about that."

All this is why the fundamental thing I do to relieve my
doubts is to sigh, "Father, I'm sorry" and drag my poor
halfheartedness to his Word and sacraments. The fundamental thing he does to relieve my doubts is to speak faith
in me through the power of his gracious Word.

The promise, "I have taken your sin away through Christ
my Son," is once again held out, once again made beautiful
in my eyes by his own Holy Spirit, and my grip is once again
tightened. My faith seems like a candle always on the verge
of going out; it has felt that way for years. Yet, fueled by an
open Bible, it remains. This smoldering wick he does not
snuff out. He does not let me forget him. My trust is kept
by the power of God,[85] and I believe in him.

There is such a place as Calvary.

There is such a Savior as Jesus.

The picture I still turn to in my mind is that of a man
crossing a river of ice on his hands and knees, spreading his

weight out as best as he can. He doesn't know how thick the ice is. Suddenly he hears a rumbling from around the river bend. It is a tractor pulling a hay wagon full of happy, screaming children past him, flat on his face . . . as if three feet of ice were going to crack at any second.

The beauty of that simple picture is that it is the ice that holds the man up. Faith is the way he walks out across it, whether tentatively or boldly—boldly is better—but it is still the ice that holds him up. And his silly thoughts about the ice do not actually change the ice. Not even a little bit. It doesn't become thin just because he thinks it is.

The ice stands for the love of God that has planned and carried out our salvation through Christ. That love simply is. Our puny doubts about God don't change him or the way he forgives us all. He doesn't love us a lot when we trust him a lot then love us a little when we trust him only a little. His faithfulness does not waver as our faith and confidence do.

"How wide and long and high and deep is the love of Christ."[86]

To trust God's gracious promises in any weak way at all, even down on all fours, is still to be saved, still to have left the shore and to have started to move across the water, which is frozen solid for your convenience. A million footprints confirm that it is safe.

"Don't you care if we drown?" a disciple shouted at Jesus. The same question was in the eyes of them all. "We're in trouble. We're barely hanging on here. . . . And you don't seem to care."

He turned away to the storm raging on the sea. "Quiet! Be still!" And she was still. The disciples were awed to see sister nature in sudden, complete submission. Jesus had made her quiet by the authority of his voice.

Then he turned around to work the same work in them, by the same power.

"Why are you so afraid? Do you still have no faith?"[87]

I pray that you suddenly realize that there's not a single answer to that question that makes any sense and that a verdict might be cast in you by the power of God's Word, a verdict you can live with.

"Believe in the Lord Jesus, and you will be saved."[88]

"There are

things I'll

never be able

to forgive"

There was a time when people could walk right up to God, look into that kind human face, and fire away. Peter's question ought to make this whole, angry world lean in close.

"How many times shall I forgive my brother? . . . up to seven times?"

It was a graceless calculation. Peter wanted to know the sensible limit to forgiveness. He was being magnanimous with his "seven times." Rabbis of the day taught that three times was plenty.

When Jesus upped the figure to "seventy-seven times," he wasn't attaching a dead statistic to a mystery so alive as forgiveness. He meant, "Peter, at seven times you're just getting warmed up."

There followed a story told by Jesus, brilliant in simplicity, which let the refusal to forgive be seen in its proper light. Jesus depicted a man, who had a legitimate gripe against another, demanding his due. A miserable beggar owed him about three months of pay-checks. If that's all we see, we say, "He has a right to be paid back. It's only fair."

But the poor man didn't have the money. If you've ever tried to talk someone out of his or her right to rage, you know what the poor man was up against. So what if the man who held his IOU got a little physical with him? A debt is a debt.

But there's more to this story. The man who was will-ing to ruin the life of another man over a debt of a few thousand dollars was himself only moments before for-given a debt of millions! He had just left the presence of sudden, unspeakable grace.

How does he look to you now?

How do you look to you when you lack the heart to forgive?

Did God forgive you seven times?

Then throw open the prison doors where all your debtors are held. For Christ's sake, release them . . . and yourself as well.

"Forgive your brother from your heart."

(Please read Matthew 18:21-35.)

It's not my proudest moment. Young and foolish, I tapped my palm to the wire of a fence I knew might be elec-trified. I watched my hand close around the wire as my muscles obeyed the irresistible impulse. Fortunately, the electricity ran in intermittent bursts, so I was able to release my grip. But for just that instant I found out what it's like to hold on to something that could kill you if you didn't let it go . . . and you knew it . . . but for the life of you, you couldn't let go.

Do you hold on to hurt? Are you a palm tightly closed around the way you were wounded? Interestingly enough, behind the New Testament Greek word for *forgiveness* is one that means "to release." That's what forgiveness is.

It's worth mentioning what forgiveness is not. You may have difficulty forgiving someone because you think for-giveness means saying that what he or she did was all right . . . a small thing after all . . . no big deal. I would never ask you to say that. The fact that we're talking about forgiveness at all means the person did something wrong to you, terribly wrong. The person should not have done it. Forgiveness means giving up the right to hurt him or her back for hurting you. Instead of anger, you offer genuine good will. That is, you let go.

You let go.

Forgiveness means pulling down the zipper on the judge's robe, slipping it off, hanging it up, leaving the matter of exacting justice to whom it properly belongs, God. Forgiveness is an act of the will, not of the emotions. It is a decision you can make even when you're still feeling bad about what was done to you. Even if someone devastated you, even if they're not sorry, you can still give the whole matter over to your God, who said, "It is mine to avenge; I will repay."[89] Leave it to him.

Yet, even understood properly, forgiveness remains an unnatural act. What comes naturally is anger. Besides being the emotional response to pain, anger is what it feels like to have something or someone get in the way of your deep desires. You can bet that a fallen world where nothing is ever quite what it's supposed to be, where something is always wrong with everything, where people are thirsting for love and meaning to degrees unavailable to them . . . well . . . it's going to be an angry place.

Sometimes it's an unnamed hostility, a bottled-up pressure inside you that is looking for someone to name as its cause. A happy dog leaves a little present on the carpet, a baby won't go back to sleep . . . and you get so angry you scare yourself.

Where did that come from?

Other times you think you know exactly why you're angry. A loved one is to blame. He is. She is. There stands the reason for your personal misery.

In any event, this hatred, this resentment, this not letting go, spiritually speaking, will kill you and everything pleasant about you. Your worst human relationship may be the one most important to pay attention to; it has destructive power. The relationship with God that you think you have in spite of all your unforgiveness, well, you don't have. Not when you hold on to your anger.

One technique for dealing with anger is called reframing. For example, a woman is angry with her mother for raising her without affection. What consumes her is how devastating that kind of childhood was on her ability to connect warmly with people. If she can "reframe" the situation, get a wider view, pull the camera back, you might say, what else might she see? She might come to empathize with her mother when she sees her mother as a frightened five-year-old shrinking away from *her* mother, who is reaching for a strap.

"Yet she never beat me," is a new thought turned loose in the daughter's mind.

Now, because her mother was abused, does that mean it was okay that the daughter was raised without affection too? No. But at least let the daughter see the whole picture. That's all I'm saying.

Jesus does something similar through that story he told about the man and the beggar. He shows us how to pull back the camera so we don't only fix our eyes on the way someone has wronged us. We see something else that is also true. My friend, each of us has a "whole picture" that includes an incomprehensible moment of release . . . a gift of staggering grace.

In a world where anger leads to anger like dominoes knocking over dominoes, God planted his cross deep into the angry ground. The crucifixion of Christ is the one fixed, unmovable spot where the aggression can end. It was the worst crime in history. The best possible man, the innocent

Son of God, was treated in the worst possible way. He was physically nailed onto wood after being scourged, beaten, spit on, laughed at . . . and, as the nails were pounded in, as it was happening, he released an unearthly fragrance:

"Father, forgive them, for they do not know what they are doing."[90]

This is God's answer to the myriad cycles of hurting and hurting back:

"I am the one whom every sin offended. I am the object of every rebellion and hurt. I am the one who holds the debt of all of you. The right to justice is mine. I am the one without sin and I can throw as many stones as I want.

"I give you my Son.

"You can walk right up and fire away. And when he dies, perhaps you will learn to feel ashamed. And when you hear that he is risen and alive, maybe then you will understand the meaning of what I have done. Oh, my children, my world, *I forgive you all!*"

You can't come into this world's story in the middle, seeing only your own life and the part you've played, and make any sense of it. Something else must be drawn within the same frame. You must not only see the wrong that was done to you, but you must pull the camera all the way back so that your eyes are also on the divine, surging wrath running through the body of Christ . . . for you. Just for you. While you think of your own forgiveness as a small thing, you will lack the power to forgive anyone else. But when you see the canceling of your own eternal debt, the doors of your prison will swing open and new, unimagined thoughts will be turned loose in your mind.

Father, forgive her. She didn't know what she was doing.

From the grace you receive, which washes over you through the Word that is "spirit and . . . life,"[91] you will have grace to give. You will become, like Jesus, a place where aggression can end.

The domino of someone's gracelessness strikes and goes no further.

In Christ the bitterness, the anger, the hate . . . they are over.

You can let go now.

He was unfaithful to her . . . and saw something die in her eyes. When he apologized, he knew not to say too much. True apologies offer no explanation, as if one were possible.

Just, "I was wrong. You didn't deserve it. There is nothing to say in my defense. I only want you to know that I'm ashamed. I want to say I'm sorry not only to you but even more to God, who wanted me to love you so much better than that."

That was many sleepless nights ago.

Now he stands by his bedroom window, looking out across the green of his own backyard, then back down to the note in his hand, feeling its influence, searching its power.

"I forgive you."

"*I'll let my kids decide for themselves*"

We see the disciples just about at their worst when, in the midst of adult concerns, they failed to recognize what mattered most. When parents were bringing little ones to Jesus to have him bless them, the Twelve ran interference.

"Now, people, you just take these little kiddies right back where you came from. . . . There you go. . . . Jesus is a busy man. . . . He doesn't have time for all these . . ."

"What are you doing?!"

There's another side to Jesus that we get to see when the children were around—his beautiful anger, his fiercely protective "Let the little children come to me," and the sudden tenderness as the hands that hold the universe dropped everything . . . for the children.

Do you want to know what it looks like when a human being, any human being, receives everything the almighty God can possibly give? How about a picture? What does it look like when someone is suddenly let in to all the love there really is?

He knelt down. He motioned for the children to come to him. They did. Chubby arms wrapped around his neck. He picked each child up one at a time, put a sacred hand on each head, and whispered something into his or her ears. Their eyes opened wide.

We don't know the message he chose for each child—what he turned loose in each child's mind, into each child's life. We just know that it was a "blessing" and that, whatever it was, they took it as true. That's what children do.

"The kingdom of God belongs to such as these."

(Please read Mark 10:13-16.)

I'll never forget taking my three-year-old along to deliver treats to some construction workers at our church building site. I admit it was intimidating stepping into the smoke-filled trailer crammed with bulky guys, me with my plate of goodies. But with one flirtatious smile, little Hannah saved me. We were a hit. At least she was. By the time we left, big carpenter hands were waving bye-bye.

One of the pleasures of having children is seeing that other side of grown-ups, the one that shows up when kids are around. Powerful men get tender. How many times have I seen that? Serious men get playful. Crude men become decent. Tight people become generous. Busy people find a little time . . . for a child. Having children means getting to see people at their finest. Sometimes.

On the other hand, grown-ups don't always shine when children are concerned. Some of the worst things that can be done, things that would devastate us one day to remember, are the things we've done to children when we have dismissed them, belittled them, hurt them. Worse, perhaps, is what we haven't done.

Did we think their spiritual needs could wait? They can't.

Do you think that if you don't give your child these beautiful Christian beliefs, they'll grow up without any beliefs at all? Ever really listen to the music on MTV and to the words being scribbled across your son's childhood?

Have you ever asked adolescents raised on this culture of ours what they believe life is for and what it all means? Did it knock the wind out of you when they said, "Nothing"? Have you ever met someone who resented her parents for meeting all her needs except the needs of her soul? "They starved me," she told me. I tried to explain that her parents were starving too.

Did you ever hear a three-year-old screaming out of a nightmare? Then you haven't forgotten what it was like. Monsters chased her in her sleep, and every instinct of yours was to run to her and give her two things: love and truth. "I've got you." "There are no monsters." Love and truth. Has it dawned on you that this is what your children want and need? What they need is you, Mom and Dad, loving them and telling them the truth.

I'm asking you to take to heart the beautiful teaching of Jesus about children. In the view of Christ, childhood is a precious thing to be embraced and protected at all cost, a fast-closing window of opportunity to impart faith to the ones who will model for us the very meaning of the word. Faith in Christ, the mystery and the miracle, is not some kind of human choice or commitment that only adults can make. The Bible has no such notion, nor that of an age of account-ability, say 13 years old, when the issues of salvation suppos-edly first matter to a human being. They matter right now to your infants as much as to you. Take a closer look at the lit-tle ones. These are not senseless brutes but little souls. Yes, they are born in the sin and darkness that we parents passed along. (You don't think so? Try putting two babies in a playpen with one stuffed dinosaur and stand back). However, when the very Spirit of God enters their hearts through the power of Baptism, saving faith is created, and human children become children of God. Real faith can live in the tiniest chil-dren by the power of the Spirit as surely as the recognition of Daddy's voice and Mommy's face does. The praise that is in them will be expressed from the moment they can form the words. And "Jesus Loves Me" on the lips of your own flesh and blood can be a piercing light in the darkness of the most cynical too-grown-up adult.

But I can still hear you saying: "Religion was jammed down my throat when I was a kid. I am not going to do that to my kids." I'm in no position to contradict you. For all I know, religion *was* jammed down your throat. Perhaps something graceless and fearful was written all over your childhood, in which case I could not agree with you more. Don't do that to your children. Thank God you've recognized it. Further, I understand that you're not consciously withholding something you know is your child's greatest need. That's why my answer is not to try to shame you— "Do you let your children decide if they're going to eat?" My answer is to help you paint that exquisite picture from Mark chapter 10 with your child in it—put the Savior's hand on your child's head and that expression of unconditional love into your child's unresisting mind: "I love you and I always will." It's what every soul is hungry for. Now, I'm just guessing here, but this religion you're concerned about not jamming down your child's throat, is it anything like that picture? No, I didn't think so.

May I tell you about my religion? Jesus blessing children is God himself revealing his heart. Yet we see his deepest expressions of love when Christ moves on from there, driven on toward one particular hill by everything you shouldn't have done but did and were supposed to do but didn't. And this kindness you see makes it safe for you to finally say, "I'm sorry" to God because for you he suffered and died. He did this for the joy it would bring him to be able to answer your sorrows with all that you've been waiting to hear—"I forgive you"—and to have it come from the One that truly has the right to say it. "I forgive you," God says with the finality of the cross, by his own body and blood.

The only thing he asks is that you take it as true, as any child would.

"Trust me," he says. You do because there's Spirit in that Word and it saves you. He says, "Come." When you do, you finally have peace. Then all of a sudden you can't think of one situation in your life that wouldn't be better if you took him as true, as a child does.

Is this the "religion" you want to be so careful not to jam . . .

No? I didn't think so.

You're going to let your children make their own decisions about religion when they're older? We're not talking about signing them up for the stewardship committee here. It's about singing songs with them in church and telling Jesus stories beside their beds. We're talking about Sunday School truths that will never leave them and little heads resting on your arms while the gracious Word steals into their souls.

"Let the little children come to me," said Jesus.

Did you ever look into a child's eyes and just love her and tell her the truth—that angels watch over her, that scarred hands dropped everything for her, that there is one face that is always turned toward her, smiling, even when she's bad?

Were you ever driving along, lost in important adult thoughts, when a three-year-old's voice from the backseat brought you back?

"I love God!"

"Me too, sweetheart."

Jesus calls his church a city on a hill that can't be hidden. But we're shown in Revelation that an earthquake will strike the city. One tenth of it will collapse. What this seems to mean is that merely being within the walls won't help certain people on the day the ground shakes.

Jesus told a story in which a fisherman examines his net. Flopping around in it are not only the good fish but some bad ones too. They're all mixed up together. Soon enough the net is pulled up into the boat. Then the sorting comes.

In another parable a farmer plants good seed in his field, but when the workers go and check on the field, they find weeds growing up with the wheat.

"Master, how could this be? You planted good seed!"

The master surveys his field, fists forming at his side. Angry tears well up.

"An enemy did this."

"Well, what should we do? Should we start pulling up the weeds?"

"No," he sighs, "no, don't do that. You'll only end up pulling up wheat as well. We'll wait until harvest. We'll sort it out then."

(Please read Matthew 13:24-30,47-52.)

A crumbling corner of the holy city, bad fish among the "keepers," weeds that sure look like wheat—different ways of saying the same thing. There are hypocrites sitting within the brick and mortar of the visible church. There are those who take up space in the building but are not part of Christ. We only need to remember the circle of 12 that Jesus himself had gathered. Within that circle was Judas, "one of the Twelve . . . who would betray him."[92] We agree with this particular objection—that there are hypocrites in the visible church—as a matter of doctrine.

Therefore, let it not be beneath the church to apologize to the world if it has failed to represent Christ. There is little to say but that the church is sorry. It is a shame when we, the people of the church, cannot point confidently to our love as the irrefutable proof of our teachings. It is a disgrace when we, the body of Christ, are unresponsive to the impulses of humility and grace that come from our Head, when our gatherings lose that quality that distinguished us from the start. What quality? The church is prodigal sons and daughters enjoying a banquet of grace, brokenhearted sinners for whom the mystery of forgiveness in the blood of the Lamb never wears off. The overwhelming emotions of the gathering are those of quiet gratitude and relief. Repentance is the inhale and exhale of this body, the perpetual breathing out of heartfelt confessions of blame and breathing in of his Word of sweet absolution. The mood is worship. What we learn when we're together is love.

Sadly, this is not what everyone will find in his or her nearest church, because all churches are not the same. A church whose whole message is, "If you keep these rules and follow these principles, God will bless you," does become something of a hypocrite factory. People feel compelled to measure up, knowing full well they had better look happy doing it. If they can't manage it, they have two options: Leave in despair or stay and pretend. Yet even within the church that has its eyes fixed on Christ crucified are those who sit there Sunday after Sunday not taking him to heart. And the fault is certainly not with Jesus or his Word, even with the church, per se. But then where does it lie?

The fault lies in what we call the sinful nature. The sinful nature refers to the way we naturally are, both those of us within the church and those who stay outside. All of us share a certain common ground overgrown with thorns. Let me take you back to the Garden of Eden, where Adam stood naked and pink before God, having done the inexcusable. It was the first time a human being ever had that experience, which is now entirely common, the experience we call shame. It's the horror of knowing yourself to be, in a word, *unacceptable.* When Adam said, "I was afraid because I was naked; so I hid,"[93] he was, in a sense, Everyman. What he feared, with good reason, was being seen as he was. His strategy was to hide, and we've been hiding ever since. Observe the gap between who we really are and the way we present ourselves to the world. Our masks, our "false fronts," are the words and manners we use to win approval or at least avoid rejection. Because if anyone would see us, they surely would reject us.

The point is that our shared sinful nature causes us to become incredibly adept at hypocrisy. We're remarkably predictable at the one great talent of our fallen personalities— perpetually putting ourselves in the best possible light. Watch yourself the next time someone questions your heart. We're so used to pretending that our true intentions are noble and good that we don't even realize we're doing it. We even fool ourselves.

Only a personal bias against the church sees hypocrisy as a particular problem in the church and not in people in general. It is a matter of Christian dogma that any human being can be false. And once you see that there's a problem with people in general, well, you're not far from understanding our Savior.

Rather than dismissing the church because of its "false sons," consider instead how it is only in a faithful church, where God's powerful Word resounds, that there is any hope of setting the masks aside. Even if some found within the church's walls don't take the Word to heart, the relevant question is this, What about those who do?

What happens to those who embrace the message of Christ in sincerity?

The harsher words of the Bible, the really terrifying ones, are designed to show us ourselves, to shake us awake to the disease of sin raging out of control within us, to burst the bubble of our vain conceit and our sense of superiority based on nothing—until we stand with Adam, bracing ourselves for the cold flood of God's rejection that ought to wash over us in waves.

Instead, what God sends is . . . Jesus.

This is the message that reaches our ears and washes over us: "I forgive you." God's own Son took our place under God's righteous wrath, as if the Son was the unacceptable one. He went there because of us, for us, instead of us, period. This is how he died.

But see, he is alive, and the gates of paradise are pushed wide open.

By this faith we find ourselves welcomed into the gracious presence of God for Jesus' sake alone. We find ourselves thoroughly known and, somehow, just as thoroughly loved. This grace penetrates the fear we hide within, and the mask falls away. When we sit in a pew under the dynamic ministry of law and gospel, we see hypocrisy for the wretched silliness it is. There is neither need nor reason to pretend anymore. We are what we are. Everyone here knows it. Taking ourselves so seriously and needing to cast ourselves in a favorable light becomes appropriately laughable, and giving up the game becomes oddly liberating. We have the unconditional acceptance of God himself in Jesus. We have the love that cannot be lost, unless we choose to walk away. God has seen us as we are and hasn't turned his face away. In Christ, he has spread his garment of grace over our nakedness. There is forgiveness here for you, just as you are.

This is the love of Christ, the love that changes us. It's the only thing that does. I don't look like much. But even when I'm a disappointment to myself, there is that something new crying within me, that something of Christ born in me, dying to be released. And one day the part you don't like about me, the part that I despise even more, will just fall away. I will see Jesus face-to-face, and I'll be like him.

May I gently suggest that it is too easy to hear and repeat the old saw, "The church is full of hypocrites." Yes, there are some who fake it. However, I cannot leave this issue behind without telling you that I would be a poor man without the people I've known in Christ. I don't want you to miss them. They are worth knowing—gracious, Christian people who don't think they're anything at all . . . just forgiven.

In a spiritually intimate moment, a man said about the congregation I was privileged to pastor, "This church is my harbor." It was mine too. Christ is still found in every word of grace spoken by a brother or sister. We believers meet one another as bringers of salvation. It is this sweet absolution that we hunger for. We talk news and shop, weather and sports. And yet, in the words of Dietrich Bonhoeffer, "the one vital thing between us . . . is Jesus"[94]—what he's done for me and what he's done for you.

I suppose what I'm really saying is this: What I love most about the Christian church is Christ.

"For where two or three come together in my name, there am I with them."[95]

"One of you will betray me," Jesus tells the Twelve.

But not one of them points to another to ask, "Lord, is it he?" Looking for hypocrisy in others is a dubious practice that is best left to God. You are just as likely to kill the wheat as to pull the weeds.

The disciples are sure enough of Jesus, and unsure enough of themselves, that each one asks, "Lord, is it I?"[96]

They are afraid of themselves, of their own natures and of what they are capable of. They look to Jesus: "If it is I, dear Lord, forgive me. Bring me back." Of all the things those men got wrong, it seems to me this is one thing they got right.

"Whatever happened to tolerance?"

Having played the role of Christ in a movie, Bruce Marchiano described what it was like getting into character. The film crew was set up in a crowded market. It could have been any seaside town in ancient Galilee where wonders once fell from the fingertips of Christ. The actor stood still in a moving sea of extras, hundreds of other actors dressed like the anonymous people of those forgotten places—Bethsaida, Korazin, Capernaum. Being "in character" meant straining to see what Jesus saw in such a crowd—not a crowd at all. There were no extras. Jesus saw each person.

In the script, taken verbatim from Matthew's gospel, was a rather prickly section titled, "Woe on Unrepentant Cities." Christ's lines ran through Marchiano's mind as the cameras were prepared.

"And you, Capernaum, will you be lifted up to the skies? No, you will go down to the depths. . . . It will be more bearable for Sodom on the day of judgment than for you."

All in an instant, the actor's composure disintegrated as the words opened up. The sea he was wading in was an awful one, a grief as big as God, an exquisite Christlike pain.

"Oh, Capernaum, no! Not you!"

Do you know the character of Jesus? Have you been to Matthew chapter 11? When countless people saw his miracles—saw him—and pretended not to notice, there came the piercing cry of a prophet torn open.

"Woe to you!"

It's not exactly tolerance, is it?

A tolerant Jesus would have said something nice and walked away. A permissive Christ wouldn't have raised the urgent questions this one did. An indulgent Lord would have thought to himself, "Do what you want. What is it to me?" After all, what is tolerance so often but apathy in a thin disguise? That, my friends, is not Jesus.

"Oh, world, no! Not you!"

(Please read Matthew 11:20-24.)

I had been invited to a discussion group at a secular college to talk about "safe sex." The leader had assured us that there was tolerance for all opinions. I made a mistake.

I believed her.

I gently tried to introduce a moral context. "I happen to believe that sexuality is a beautiful gift from God and that it has purposes no one has mentioned yet . . ." So it was that the most vicious verbal assault I have ever received as a soft-spoken Christian came in the name of tolerance.

Tolerance is a lovely word applied to nonmoral issues—the color of your skin, the delicious and mysterious flavor of your culture and ethnicity, the way your history has shaped you differently than mine has shaped me. These are beautiful to me. That you think differently than I do fascinates me, like an open window does. I do want to know and see who you are. Why don't we all speak openly, listen generously, and get along?

There are moral issues, however, such as those that surround the value of human life, the family, and human sexuality. Here our talk of tolerance stops making sense. You say, "Who am I to make a judgment?" Listen to yourself, however, when you are the victim of someone's infidelity. Moral ambiguity vanishes like smoke, and you give yourself away.

"How dare he do that to me!"

In real life you experience moral outrage as permissiveness gives way to honest disgust. Words like *should not* and *wrong* are not so easy to banish from our vocabulary. Finally, if we do stop calling anything bad, we'll lose our ability to call anything good—such as integrity or courage—or at least to mean anything when we do. Esteeming virtues such as these doesn't reflect well on liars and pleasant cowards.

But wait. Isn't Jesus all about forgiveness and tolerance?

Forgiveness, yes. *Tolerance,* no. The words are miles apart.

If you think of Jesus as the warm, fuzzy, flannel-graph character that always had a sweet thing to say, think again. Certainly his tenderness with sinners is legendary. Read the gospels, however, and you'll also encounter one whose severity with sinners leaves you speechless. He is the pristine expression of God's own character. He embodied both love and holiness, holding both perfectly, each at full strength. He can neither say that he doesn't care about us, nor that he doesn't care what we do, and still be Jesus. In Chesterton's metaphor, Jesus is brilliant crimson set beside dazzling white, not an unmanly blend of pink.[97]

To insist on tolerance for every behavior imaginable is to be mistaken about God on both counts. Once you wake up to the God who is infinitely more holy than you realize, you will realize he is infinitely more loving than you knew as well. He found a way to remain both the fiercest judge and the most tender Savior at the same time, each to an inexpressible degree.

First of all, God is a blazing fire of perfect justice. I wonder how many objections to Christianity arise from the

simple failure to face the horror of human sin and its con-
sequences. We watch the latest example of human depravity on the evening news with precious little understanding:
we human beings are all cut from one cloth. What's wrong
with them is also wrong with us. We are the rebellious,
still-falling race. To see that is to understand why the holiness of a good God cried out what he did through the
ancient prophets. God would gather all humanity into one
terrible spot to condemn it and destroy it.

Where is the love?

Who could have imagined that the "one terrible spot"
would be the body and soul of his one and only Son? The
crucifixion of Jesus Christ, the Son of God, involved an
unthinkable substitution. "God made him who had no sin to
be sin for us."[98] The cross of Christ is the place where humanity was both judged and saved, put to death and given life,
completely condemned and even more thoroughly loved.
God's obligation to answer human depravity with punishing
indignation and his deeper compulsion to pardon and rescue
us met in the crucifixion of his one and only Son.

Who can fathom that when sinful humankind and its holy
God met, it was the holy God who withered and died? But
first he shouted, "It is finished."[99] This is not the feeble
voice of tolerance—What is it to me what you do or what
you are?—but the breathtaking sound of forgiveness, full
and free, for the entire world.

When I write about the issues along the cultural divide—
divorce, abortion, extramarital sex, homosexuality—and call
them evil, you reply, "Isn't God a forgiving God?" Do you
mean that? Do you want forgiveness? Are you acknowledg-
ing such things as the sins you personally abhor? Do you
desire both God's mercy and his help to overcome sin? Then
I offer you the best possible news. I answer with an unequiv-
ocal "Yes, God forgives" and say, "Let us speak further
about Jesus."

However, it is hypocrisy to stake your claim on a merciful God without admitting that it's precisely mercy that you need. God is also holy. "It is a dreadful thing to fall into the hands of the living God."[100] This is the aspect of God you will encounter one day if you do not repent. It is terrifying to contemplate.

Do I enjoy writing those words? Friend, what would you have me say to you? It's no fun playing the prophet, being the one who is awake and who sees, who watches the world go on being the world and feels like crying. I see the victims of society's "victimless crimes." From illicit sex the children keep coming who will never know their daddies. Consenting adults keep sharing their deadly diseases. Mothers keep choosing death for their unborn children, while empty arms go right on aching for little ones. Full of years, people at the door of eternity are offered death drugs instead of my living Jesus.

These are scenes of tragedy along the slippery slope. At the bottom is a very real hell.

There is a better path.

"Follow me," said the smiling Christ, his face shining like the sun.

Christians are the ones called to speak for him according to his inspired Word. I must not be the kind of Christian you approve, the pleasant coward who never dares to disrupt you on your way to disaster.

I am to make you hear the harder parts of Scripture as they are meant to be heard—make you hear the law as if there were no gospel. Just once consider the holiness of God without a flippant, "Yeah, but he forgives." As a little girl once said, "Jesus didn't have to come, you know."

She's right. He didn't.

"The soul that sins is the one that will die," declares the Lord. That truth stares you in the face. Show me, please, some glimmer of recognition.

And I will give you gospel as if there is no law, for the law has been nailed to a cross.

I will hold out to you grace without condition.

I will show you Jesus.

A teenager told me, "My parents don't care what I do." She seemed to like it that way. "They don't care where I go. They don't care when I get home." But there was a sadness about her, just the same, as if the truth was already sinking in.

"My parents . . . don't care."

This is not what God is like. Not even a little bit.

He cares what you do, what you are, and what you are to become.

Because he cares about you.

More than you know.

A majestic peak just across the northern border of Israel, Mount Hermon affords a panoramic view of the Promised Land. Jesus and his intimate circle—Peter, James, and John—climbed to this place he had chosen.

There was something he wanted to show them.

Like the sun finding a sudden opening in a cover of clouds, the glory burst out from his human face. His clothes became "dazzling white." The signal of the almighty God's presence in the wandering days of the Hebrews, the *Shekinah* cloud, embraced them all. For the second time, the Father abandoned his restraint.

"This is my Son, whom I love. Listen to him!"

Jesus was showing the friends he had made who he is, giving them something to remember while they watched him die. It was a combination of events— really seeing Christ and seeing him really crucified—that Peter would never quite get over.

But there was one interesting moment after the glory was hidden back inside the flesh. Jesus' face looked like any face again and his clothes like any clothes. As they were walking down the mountain, Jesus "gave them orders not to tell anyone" about what they had just witnessed until after he had "risen from the dead."

It is here that we are treated to the sight of Peter, James, and John discussing what "rising from the dead" could possibly mean. They scratched their heads and searched out an interpretation of the deep, dark, mysterious words.

"I will be crucified"—I wonder what he means by that.

"I will be put to death and be buried"—What do you suppose he's driving at?

"On the third day, I will rise to life"—Sorry, Jesus, but you're losing me.

So it went. The light shined into the darkness so that the night was like the day, but the darkness just could not understand.

(Please read Mark 9:2-10.)

An audience member made the mistake of starting a sentence with, "The Bible says . . ." Oprah was unusually abrupt: "I don't pretend to know what that book means." That is a simple way to derail a conversation about spiritual things should the conversation venture too close to home. "That's your interpretation. Other people, who are as knowledgeable as you, take it differently." The Christian camp is so fraught with disagreement that it becomes all too convenient to dismiss Christianity entirely. Who can say what's right?

The issue of interpreting Scripture is an important one and the question, How do I know it means what you say it means? is legitimate. In fact, all human language inherently requires interpretation. We are very accustomed to the mental process of assigning meaning to the communication we receive. We are always asking quite unconsciously, What does the speaker or the writer intend? Does that mean we complain that human words are hopelessly unclear and not worth the trouble? Hardly. What else do we really have, besides words, that answers our hunger to connect with one another, to have something within me be known to you? We plan to keep using words and will keep expecting that others will understand us well enough.

There is nothing nonsensical about the notion that God, who created us to communicate with words, would do so with us. Certainly many people in this world "wag their own tongues and yet declare, 'The LORD declares.'"[101] They should be ashamed of themselves. But these abuses do not somehow negate the fact that some words really *are* divine. From God's deep desire to be known by us—so rich in his mercy—he has spoken to our race in a way we are able to understand, that is, in words. The point in all of this is that you are not to think of the matter of interpreting Scripture as some sort of mystical art that is inherently different from the interpretation of language in which you engage every day.

The fact that God has condescended to communicate with us by the medium of human language does not somehow invite a "whatever it means to you" approach, but precisely the opposite. We are to keep asking about biblical revelation, What does God mean to say through the human authors who were "carried along by the Holy Spirit"?

Is this or that part of the Bible figurative or literal, symbolic or plainspoken fact? I often ask people who are bothered by questions like these to come up with everyday examples. When was the last time someone was speaking to you and you were left in the dark wondering if their words were a figure of speech or intended literally? I suppose it happens . . . but not very often. Similarly, the preponderance of the Scriptures, should you dare to actually read them, reads something like this: "The wages of sin is death, but the gift of God is eternal life in Christ Jesus our Lord."[102] What is there to figure out? It's really very clear.

That may be the real problem people have. Mark Twain commented that what he found disturbing about the Bible was not the things he didn't understand but the things he did. While I cheerfully admit that the Bible leaves some questions open, they aren't the main ones. And the overall message of God's Word is not in any serious doubt. A dismissal such as, "That's just your interpretation" can be a thinly disguised evasion of the plain meaning of the words, an unholy smoke screen in which to hide simple unbelief.

The words are all too clear. People refuse to believe them.

Assuming your question about interpretation is an honest one, we can talk about the serious study of biblical interpretation, or hermeneutics. We can derive certain principles of interpretation that responsibly handle the Word of God as it deserves to be handled. For the first and best example of these principles, it only makes perfect sense to let "Scripture interpret Scripture." Prophetic or symbolic verses, or verses open to more than one interpretation, are understood in the light of simple and crystal clear verses. Great care is given that no point of established doctrine is left to hang only on just one or two difficult verses. Any particular topic is exhaustively studied by gathering every relevant verse from throughout the Scriptures, allowing all these verses to speak as one. In these and in other ways, we mean to allow God to be his own interpreter. For our part, our intention is to believe the single, simple sense of each sentence he has graciously revealed to us in his Holy Word.

Now, a hostile reader can pick a fight at every biblical street corner and can willfully interpret any number of verses in ways that make the Bible seem to be a tangle of contradiction. (You can play the same games in any conversation if you are so minded, though you do it to your own loss.) Wear a more humble frame of mind, in a posture of readiness to learn and receive, and you will discover that the same Scriptures can be read quite naturally in a way that lets you perceive the coherence from Genesis to Revelation. To never once do so, to never allow the Bible to speak to you in its own uncanny, disturbing, consoling voice, is to slap off the lights, draw the blinds, leave your mail on the counter unopened . . . and don't dare answer the phone.

And when you say, "Ah, but do you really take the Bible literally?" as if we should all know better than that by now, I answer that I do. And this is what I take the term *literal* to mean: the literal interpretation takes the Bible as it plainly asks to be taken in any given context. By taking every Scripture at face value, by studying sentences in their contexts, by exhausting the meanings of the words according to their usages in other places and the grammatical constructions in which they are found, we are always after the author's intended meaning. (Please distinguish this use of the term *literal* with being literalistic. That is to say, I certainly do allow for the countless times the biblical authors write in parable form and employ poetic imagery and colorful figures of speech.) What emerges from the literal interpretation is a startlingly lucid book about salvation in Jesus Christ.

Then why so many denominations? Notice three things about the various Christian camps. First, recognize that when there are stark differences in their teachings, these do not come from some supposed ambiguity in the Bible but from each denomination's different views about how far and how seriously to take what the Bible actually says. One of the claims the Word of God makes for itself is that it is a clear book, "a lamp to my feet and a light for my path."[103] However, when a theological system means to balance the Bible with human reason, tradition, or experience as equal authorities, it arrives at a different place than I do when I let the Scripture stand apart as the only infallible source of truth. Further, any verse of Scripture can cause a parting of the ways when one Christian accepts its intended meaning and another does not because of personal biases and theological assumptions.

All of this is a human problem—we seek other lights to guide us. Better, it's a spiritual problem—when will we trust him? The problems this whole chapter addresses always lay within us, never in the flawless Word of God.

Second, please don't say that the differences among denominations are arguments about nothing. Is there grace to be found for my baby girl in that simple water and Word that is Holy Baptism? Disagree with my joyful yes if you must, but don't say it doesn't matter. It matters to her as few things in her life ever will. Beneath the disagreements between church bodies that can seem petty from the outside are matters of profound spiritual importance. "Christ crucified" remains a jarring offense to human reason—that the gift could be so free, or that it had to be—therefore human ideas gain easy entrance into the places Christians gather. Salvation that is by grace alone, through faith alone, slips so easily from the human mind, as soon as the Word of God does. Strings are always being tied to unconditional grace. When these strings attached are seen for what they are, the honorable thing and the thing that can bless all who listen is graceful disagreement. For that matter, stand up and holler if that's what is necessary to make Christ known.

Third, do not naïvely dismiss the "immensely formidable unity"[104] of Christendom across the world and across the ages. Though there are differences among Christian groups, notice the vast and beautiful common ground among all those who have ever recognized the Bible as "the very words of God."[105] In other words, have no doubt that the Holy Trinity, the true divinity of Christ and his full humanity, his atoning death on the cross, his resurrection from the dead, and the forgiveness of sins are clearly revealed truths that are there for the taking by anyone who opens God's book and takes it at face value.

"You will do well to pay attention to it, as to a light shining in a dark place."[106]

Yes, Scripture requires interpretation. But has it occurred to you that life itself requires far more? Questions hide beneath questions as we struggle to assign the true meanings to shame, misery, and death. We don't know what life means, until God himself pierces our darkness.

"This is my Son, whom I love. . . . Listen to him!"[107]

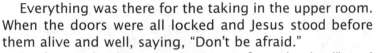

Everything was there for the taking in the upper room. When the doors were all locked and Jesus stood before them alive and well, saying, "Don't be afraid."

So this is what he meant by "rising from the dead"! And Peter, James, and John finally saw the light. They saw the only hope, the only peace, the only joy when they saw Jesus alive.

So this is what he meant.

"Religion is a crutch for the weak"

Did you ever see your father cry when you were a child? Did you watch wide-eyed his grown-up shoulders tremble and his face sink into his hands? It was profoundly unsettling, in the way an earthquake is. That which nothing could shake, the very ground beneath your feet, was shaking. That's the look and feel of the moment in the gospels when Jesus was preparing to die, when the One who holds all things together seemed to be coming apart. What is this cracking you hear in the voice of God?

"My soul is overwhelmed . . ." is the kind of thing I say, not God. And the words are repeated in the eyes that see every awful thing, those burdened, plaintive eyes.

"[I am] overwhelmed with sorrow to the point of death. Stay . . . with me."

Not since Bethlehem has Jesus seemed so small as this. As he braced for a weakling's death on a humiliating cross, unspeakably alone, he actually seemed to lean on the likes of Peter, James, and John.

But make no mistake. This weakness was a chosen weakness. It was our weakness that he found a way to share. It was our trembling in the face of dreadful things like death and hell—things no human being can handle—that was undoing him.

So effortlessly could he have pushed back the coming pain. Within any moment during that day, it would have been nothing for him to unveil the glory he hides—after the first ripping of the scourge . . . after the twenty-first . . . when a soldier held the first nail . . . and took his measure with the hammer . . . at any moment.

But where would that have left us?

The weakness of Christ just happens to be the flexing of a power beyond our wildest dreams. This is what it looks like when God loves us in the muscular, mighty way he loves us. The One with the power to call 12 legions of angels to his instant defense has something else more spectacular still.

The power *not* to.

(Please read Matthew 26:36-38.)

George Carlin once appeared on "Larry King Live" to explain that Christianity is a crutch, that all it really amounts to is a pure invention for weak, pathetic people. A rather grating comedian stands on the outside of the mystery—the only peace I've ever known, the only hope—and announces to the world that he, George Carlin, has seen to the center of it, has gotten to the bottom of it, and can tell us "all it really is." Apparently he has the omniscience to explain my own thinking to me and the real reason I believe.

I *need* to believe because I'm weak.

May I start by pointing out how many objections to Christianity are not really objections at all? "Religion is a crutch for the weak" is a potshot that entirely skirts the issue. (There are other examples: "You are Christian because you were born into it, and it's been poured down your throat. If you were raised Hindu, you would be Hindu." I can just as easily say that the religion of secular-

ism has been poured down your throat, especially if you
come from the same culture I do.) All I'm saying is that
you should be on the lookout for the many times refutation
is no part of the argument being made. See how Carlin
evades the central question that is posed by the boggling
design of our world, the miracle of its existence, the tragic
nature of humanity, the phenomenon of Holy Scripture,
the deafening testimony from Jesus' own time and place,
the most natural interpretation of all the historical data we
have, the uniqueness of Christ himself as the compelling
power behind the greatest movement in history, and so on.
And not he or anyone else can suggest an anti-theistic sce-
nario to explain it all better than faith does.

What is the real question being so carefully stepped
around when you say, "Religion is a crutch for the weak"?
Is Christianity true?

A man wishing to dismiss the experience of millions as
fit for derision reaches for the most damning weapon he
can find—and it is the fact that this faith has been giving
strength to weak people for two thousand years, which,
interestingly enough, is just what we would expect it to do
IF IT WERE TRUE!

I look again and look closer at George Carlin, and
although he means to rob me of everything I can truly call
mine, the anger drains out of me. He's not getting any
younger. For the man who asked Larry King, "Why can't
we make fun of Christians?" the questions will all change in
time. The truth is, for all his false bravado, there are things
in this world he can't handle. None of us can. In addiction
clinics and hospital morgues, in nursing homes and funeral
homes are the hints of things that are bigger than we are.
Our guilt and our death, the stench of our failures to love,
the shame of our naked corpses, the very real judgment of
God—before such things we are not merely weak, we are
nothing at all.

A person can live an entire life around the question, Am I enough? "Am I adequate to face whatever life will send?" we ask, hungry for any evidence we can scrounge out in the affirmative. People daily enter the world, driven to validate the space they have taken up and to avoid the verdict "Not enough." But nothing could be clearer than the essential inadequacy of humanity. If we would try for a single hour to be holy—to think not of ourselves or any impure thing— we would see what weakness is. There is not one thing we can do to make our lives wind up any differently than they will. We are going to die. We are utterly powerless when it comes to the things we care about most, and we are going to die. George, the questions will change.

"My life . . . it runs out . . . O God . . . what now?"

Philip Yancey observed that in Old Testament times, when God provided the very kinds of evidence George Carlin demands—when the Lord showed up and left the scorch marks behind—it didn't result in the things God desires.[108] Remarkably, people did not trust him or love him in any lasting way. They remained breathtakingly immature. Our faith and our love—the two things God says are all that matter[109]—are the very things he doesn't win by sheer brute force. The pyrotechnic displays of raw power only made the ancient people cringe and run away. "But I," Jesus cried to a stunned crowd, "when I am lifted up from the earth, will draw all men to myself."[110]

In that lifting up that was the crucifixion of Christ, God made himself unthinkably weak. By this surrendering death, he has saved us all. We take our first tentative steps toward him, drawn in by the sight of emptied-out omnipotence and glory blown out like a candle. The Spirit empowers words such as "Come to me, all you who are weary . . ."[111] and we meet at the cross a God we trust because "when we were still powerless, Christ died for the ungodly."[112] This is the God we do love . . . for loving us first.

There are answers we cannot find except in the scattered pieces of our imagined self-sufficiency. We still ask, "Am I enough?" with so much of our natural life emanating out of fear of the answer. But there are things we'll never know until the answer comes back no. We may need to fall in whatever way we fear the most to find it is not at all what we thought . . . because we are caught by Christ. It is then that we come to feel the cords of love tighten, the ones that had been holding us all along. Then we come to know the strength of his hands. This is strength: when the exquisite words of the prophets and apostles at last become our own, the very thing we are longing to say to God: "Whom have I in heaven but you? And earth has nothing I desire besides you."[113] Nothing else even makes sense. A peace comes to us that no one can explain. One of his Hebrew names is *El Shaddai,* which means "the God who is enough." For every new inadequacy we are made to see in ourselves, there is always some new sufficiency to be found in him, and the finding is worth it all.

My many weaknesses are toothpick-sized slivers in places I can't . . . quite . . . reach. I've cried, "Jesus take them away, and see how I will serve you." But then I understand that the world doesn't need another display of self-sufficiency. It has plenty of "strong" people to look at. Let me offer something else to look at entirely: what it looks like to rely on Christ, if even to get up in the morning.

Learn how weaknesses can be befriended. Don't merely accept them; celebrate them and make them your boast. Throw your head back and laugh when you discover what the saying means, "When I am weak, then I am strong."[114]

You see, Jesus loves us. That is enough.

There is an astonishing release of Spirit and strength that occurs at the weak and broken places. A mother blinded by grief for the child she has lost still sees Christ. She wonders, "How long until I see him in heaven?" A high school boy begs of God, "Can you make me more like Jesus?" A woman in a nursing home with nothing left at all asks me, "Why, of all people, am I so blessed?" Through Christ, the questions change.

"The weak . . . renew their strength. . . . They will soar on wings like eagles; they will run and not grow weary, they will walk and not be faint."[115]

"Why doesn't he answer my prayers?"

In the Garden of Gethsemane, from just a stone's throw away, watch Jesus pray. You see Jesus fallen, his face in the dirt. You hear God crying out to God. You wonder, "What could it be that God, wrapped in flesh, wants so badly that he bleeds?"

First, he wants there to be a way around the cross—and don't be disturbed. There is nothing about sinless perfection that says he ought to want the experience of crucifixion or ought to want nails through his hands and feet. He will receive within himself the accumulated guilt of this whole human race. He will feel in his soul the Father's face turning away. The very thought makes him so sad he could die.

"Father, if you are willing, take this cup from me."

Second, he wants his Father's will to be done—that the people of the world should be redeemed whatever the cost, that though undeserving we should yet know the breathtaking love of his Father, that we should be let in to that love and see with our eyes the glory Christ had before the creation of the world.

The dreadful truth dawns. The answers to both his prayers can't be yes. His deep yearnings are incompatible. Either he will die horribly or we will—one or the other is certain. Either his need will be met or ours.

Which, dear Lord? You're going to have to lead us to the bottom of your desire. Which do you crave more?

"Father . . . not my will, but yours be done."

That's what you hear from Jesus, from a stone's throw away.

(Please read Luke 22:39-44.)

There's a logic we find invincible in our pain. Since there is a God of absolute power loving me perfectly—he can do anything and says he would do anything for me—there's a simple way to test it. It's called prayer.

There's a hurting little girl who prays to feel better. You say, "I know what I'd do if I were God. How does he resist?" How many people have laid out that seemingly obvious test? They sent up a prayer and riding on that prayer was, "Let's see if it makes sense to believe in him." How many people walk away from the door of religion concluding there's no one on the other side because "He didn't answer me"?

I must interject that it's only by faith in Christ that any sinner even has a relationship with God. If you pray to a god whose love is bought by good works, for example, I'm not surprised that there was nobody home. That god doesn't exist. If you are praying in Jesus' name, relying on the perfect access Christ has granted you to the very Father in heaven, he has certainly heard every prayer, not to mention every inward groan and barely audible sigh. Knowing Jesus means leaving out any thought of *making* God willing to listen. By faith in Jesus, God's heart is already entirely yours. He hears you.

And his answer is often yes. He may grant the very thing you requested at the perfect time or give something you will admit was better by far. Let the seasoned believers around you share their stories of answered prayer. You may be astounded, and you may learn a few things about how to pray. "I will not let you go unless you bless me,"[116] cried Jacob in the Old Testament. "Lord, you'll give up before I do," was the tenacious spirit of his striving with God. Think of Jesus teaching his disciples "that they should always pray and not give up."[117]

Indeed, think of Jesus. Think of the cross. If for a time God doesn't seem to care, know him better than that.

But what about the times when no answer comes? Consider Jesus. So close to the center of the story of our faith is the unanswered prayer of God's dearly loved Son. Four things are crystal clear:

The Father loved his Son.

The Son did not want the horrifying agony of the cross.

The Son prayed to the Father until sweat like blood appeared on his forehead.

Still the cross.

What are we missing? Where does our logic break down when we're so sure we know what a God of love should do about a heartfelt prayer? Consider three simple truths that might bring an appropriate humility to our questions.

1. The answer to all our prayers can't be yes. What one person prays for may not be compatible with another person's prayers. If two men pray for one woman's heart, at least one will be disappointed. It's that kind of world.

Also, I may not be aware of the inconsistencies among my own prayers. There are my prayers to be happy, my prayers to be good, and circumstances in which both cannot take place. "Lord, let me be popular" doesn't jibe with "Help me speak the truth." It's that kind of world too.

So may I mention one prayer that lets us put our hands to the rope the Father has been pulling since time began?

May we have ears to hear a billion believers across time praying in perfect harmony that which the Spirit of Christ has moved us to long for as well: "Our Father who art in heaven . . ."

2. We don't know what should happen. God knows the future and the past. He knows everything—every fact right now and every result tomorrow of every conceivable contingency today. He is the only one who knows. We don't know the first thing about what is good or bad for us. Take the example of Jesus' disciples. What do you imagine they might have prayed for before they fell asleep in Gethsemane? That Jesus would snap out of it? (He had frequently spoken about dying and was obviously distressed.) I can imagine them praying that they could have a pleasant night, a nice Passover in Jerusalem, and then a safe journey back to Galilee. Clearly if they could have undone, through their prayers, the events that began to unfold next, they would have . . . and so they would have prayed to be alone and lost, in pain and in the dark forever. If God had said yes to those prayers, that's where they would have been. They didn't know what was good or bad for their own circumstances.

Neither do we. A Christian man stood beside the casket of his little boy and said to me, "God took my son when I was still his hero." He was thinking of the many things fathers and sons go through that he and his son would never know. It was a remarkable moment, but don't misunderstand. It didn't mean his heart wasn't breaking. It didn't mean he would ever have chosen to be standing beside that casket on such a sunny day. He was forcing himself to admit that he didn't know where the path would have led on from there, should things have happened differently. All he knew was that he had a son in heaven. He was betting his soul that it made sense to trust in Christ, that he would see his son again and that they would stand side by side one day shouting, "My God has done all things well!"

I don't know what will happen in the story God has written for my life. But I do know him through his Son, Jesus. With eyes fully open, I want him to be God, not me. I want his will to be done.

3. We're only dimly aware of what we really want. The soul thirsts for God as a deer pants for water. Though we don't know it by nature, it is God and only God who could ever match the depth of our thirst for love and meaning. In this way, you can trace any of our desires back to the Source. The prayer behind all our prayers is for the One who fills everything in every way, who loves us even though he knows us. I've prayed to be taller, smarter, and better. I've prayed for success, for love, for wisdom. What I've always really wanted was God.

That's what makes my sin such a dreadful thing. Sin put the one thing my heart really longed for far beyond my resources and reach. The sin of us all cut us off from Life and Love, and it would have cut us off forever . . . but we found all we ever really wanted clawing in Gethsemane's dirt.

There was Jesus saying yes to the prayer behind all our prayers.

He was giving himself away, making a way for us to go home, whatever the cost to himself. If his will includes doing that for me, and it does, then what can I say?

"May his will be done."

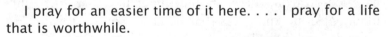

I pray for an easier time of it here. . . . I pray for a life that is worthwhile.

I pray for some circumstance to go the way I want. . . . I plead to my God that I want to know his Son.

I pray to be happy here in this or that way. . . . . I pray, "Father, let me see your face in heaven."

To each of these the Father in heaven must say, "Which is it?" and I remember what I really want. I don't want to stay standing a stone's throw away from Jesus.

"Your will be done."

"Where is God when I'm hurting?"

"Put your sword away," he says to Peter. "Shall I not drink the cup my Father has given me?"

Before long his torn back is laid on the wood. A soldier holds a fistful of nails, while sitting on his chest. Someone offers him a cup. It's gall, a narcotic mixture designed to dull his senses and take the edge off his pain.

Try to imagine this moment. The spikes are about to be driven in. Jesus takes a sip of the gall, realizes what it is, spits it out, and turns his head away. He's got to be alert for his crucifixion. He's not going to miss any of what is to come. He doesn't want the edge taken off. He wants to drink the cup the Father has given him.

The Son of God snapping his head away from the wine vinegar—burn this picture into your mind. See him drinking us to the bottom, all the sin of each of us. Witness that resolve to drink the entire cup.

It was from his Father.[118]

(Please read Matthew 27:32-40.)

Many words have been thrown at the problem of personal suffering in an attempt to make sense out of it. Precious few reach the people actually doing the suffering. Much of what gets said in hospital rooms, such as, "Maybe if you were right with God this wouldn't be happening to you," manages to make things worse.

At the exact center of the Christian faith, however, is an answer of another kind entirely. Unique among the images set before the pained eyes of the hurting is that of Jesus on the cross he chose to bear.

A trickle of red down the side of God's face.

The Lord Almighty come close enough, made small enough, to get hurt.

Where is God when I'm hurting? Let all who ask that question consider the crucifixion of Christ—God drawn so near to a suffering world as to actually ask the same question himself in the midst of unimaginable torment.

"My God, my God, why have you forsaken me?"[119]

He shared our flesh. He understands our pain. He saw the universe through blurring human tears. He even participated with us in asking, "Why?"

On a television drama called *Judging Amy,* a woman who has given up on God catches up with her friend on his way into church. "Come inside," he says. But she stands on the church steps wanting to know why. When things don't work out, when life hurts so badly, it just doesn't seem to make sense.

She pleads: "I don't understand! How can you believe in him?"

He fumbles for words. "Sometimes you just have to give God the benefit of the doubt."

"Why should I do *that?*"

So he talks about his baby girl, what it's like to hold her, what new thoughts come to him as he's looking at her.

"God gave me this child. There's a lot I don't understand. But I understand this."

I'm walking my mind down a similar path, not remembering my own children but Isaiah's prophecy: "Unto us a child is born, unto us a Son is given."[120] I'm thinking of one perfect boy born in Bethlehem—the first movements of God, out of glory, reaching for a suffering world toward us and our pain in a way barren explanations never could.

God gave me this child.

I'm thinking of him who did not deserve to suffer and all of the reasons I do. I'm letting the gruesome reality of crucifixion settle into my soul. What human sights and sounds would accompany the driving of nails through a human hand? What was written across his face? I'm remembering who this One is. I'm turning the words over in my mind. "I go to prepare a place for you . . ."[121]

There's a lot I don't understand. But I understand this.

I don't give God the benefit of the doubt. I trust him outright. He won that much from me when he saved me. What he and his powerful words accomplish in those who know Christ is the gentle turning away from the bitter "Why?" We learn to ask better questions, questions that point ahead and lead us through.

"What good purposes can God be working out through suffering?" we ask, and the answers start to come. Suffering reduces us down to our need. Pain turns our faces around if we had forgotten him. We grip the Word because we have to . . . or is the deeper fact that his Word grips us?

"Our light and momentary troubles are achieving for us an eternal glory that far outweighs them all."[122]

It is glistening words like those by the Spirit of Christ that make all the difference. Without them we are prone to make suffering a cause of bitterness and to give in to despair. When we embrace the Word of God and grip it with all the energy that pain provides, we receive only good for all our tears.

We learn more of him and the mystery of his love when we are in the dark, when that Word is the only light, than we ever could in worldly daylight. I know that what I've learned of Christ is worth suffering in every way. Faith refined in the fire of suffering is better than gold. It's my ticket home.

Pain tells us that we aren't home yet. The aching keeps us from being satisfied with this world. We aren't in Eden anymore. We won't be right until our feet touch heaven. Indeed, suffering has a way of keeping us awake and longing for the only things that will satisfy us, the one person, the only place. Until we're there, seeing him face-to-face, we must groan our perpetual, inward, *"Abba."* "Ah, Father."

He hears us. He is on his way. Then comes joy.

Consider how the exhilaration of the runner breaking the tape has everything to do with the agony he endured as he ran. The joy does not come in spite of the pain but because of it. That inseparable connection between pain and joy is written largely in the beautiful fact of heaven. Heaven is a gift so vast and of such a kind that it reaches back and redeems every last thing we endured. We'll call it all joy as we stand in heaven and shout, "God has done all things well."

The pain now is part of the joy then.

Further, confronted by suffering, we can learn to ask, "What is my response?" Our faithful reaction to pain—we answer with trust and we answer with love—is the blessing otherwise unknown. When suffering poses the eternally significant question, Is God worthy of my faith even now? all of heaven waits for my answer. I say he is. When I am confronted, appropriately enough, with my small share of this world's pain, let me say with Christ, "Shall I not drink the cup the Father has given me?"[123]

"Drinking our cup" means more than grudgingly accepting our lives. It means befriending and embracing our reality—all of it—because it's from our Father, who happens to love us.[124] "Drinking our cup" means looking for the unique potential to know God, to reflect him, and to be blessings in these lives we were given. Not different ones. Our lives right now.

I take my first sips as I savor the memory of searching for Jesus in a lonely time, and I begin to understand the strength that is found in weakness. I don't just make the best of it, but I am as thankful for the bad as for the good. I look around and realize that not every life lived in this world includes a moment of finding God. Not every path ends up in him. This one does . . . and I want this to be my life.

My cup overflows.

Finally, the pain around us provides the opportunities for us to respond, to be Jesus to hurting people, to cry with them as he does, to love them as he does. It is never mean- ingless suffering when someone's pain hurts us too . . . and we reach out a Christlike hand. We stand pleading on the steps of the church God bought with his own blood.

"Come inside."

Dr. James Dobson shares a very instructive moment from his personal life.

The doctor asked Dobson to hold his little boy from behind so he could scrape around in his infected ear with a sharp instrument. This Dobson did . . . barely. Each time the doctor started, the child exploded in pain.

Father and son happened to be positioned in front of a mirror so that they could see each other's faces. The father met his son's eyes. They were screaming, "How can you do this to me? How you can hold me down when it hurts so bad?"

Years later, Dobson struggled for composure as he talked about that day. There were neither words to express how much he loved this child, nor words to explain the necessary pain to the satisfaction of that little boy.

There was no way to make him understand. His father could only hold him. He could only let his own heart break, let the sorrow in his own eyes be his answer. "I do love you."

This is what I believe about pain.

I believe that there are things we aren't equipped to understand, that the explanation we demand wouldn't make "all better." But I think of that moment in the doctor's office between that father and his child. And I believe that the cross of Christ is just such a revealing of the love in the Father's heart. I believe that the promises from there are just such a holding.

Drops of blood dotted the forehead of Christ that night.

He had been praying.

Suddenly he stood up and strode to the entrance of the Garden of Gethsemane, a move John will later describe in one of the most chilling sentences in the Bible: "Jesus, knowing everything that was coming upon him . . ." Knowing everything—knowing "to the very last detail." Soldiers arrived to arrest him, as if on cue, hundreds of heavily armed men, as if they expected a fight, carrying torches, as if they expected to be searching the bushes. He was not what they expected.

"Who is it you want?"

"Jesus of Nazareth."

"I AM."[125]

With that several hundred men, Judas among them, fell backward to the ground before Majesty and the sound of God speaking his own name. Jesus stood there bathed in the light of a full moon, the expression on his face unchanged.

"Who is it you want?"

Soldiers and guards struggled to their feet, trying to regain their dignity, but their minds were spinning! What had just happened? The captain could only say again, "Jesus of Nazareth."

Again he answered, "I AM . . . and you will let these men go."

It was not a request, not a bargain. It was a direct command.

Peter, however, didn't want to be "let go," not after all his boasting. He drew a short sword from the folds of his garment. "Shall I fight for you?" he cried, not waiting for an answer. Instead he slashed at the servant Malchus, severing a small piece of his ear. It was a show of love by Peter but a poor one, one that ignored everything Jesus stood for.

Hundreds of swords must have flashed at that moment. Jesus moved quickly to save Peter's life, not wanting him to die by the very weapon he had drawn.

"Put your sword away!"

Jesus knelt down beside the whimpering Malchus; blood seeped out between his enemy's fingers. And in a scene of dark chaos, violence, and maddening injustice, this divine act of human kindness.

Jesus healed him.

(Please read John 18:1-11.)

You see the flaws of the Christian church? So do I. I have taken off the rose-colored glasses. I don't love the church as one who has never really seen her. I have seen her. And I do. So what do I say to this challenge: "The church has done terrible things"?

People point to the war she waged with unbelievers during the Crusades, the heretics she burned in the Middle Ages, or the times the church has been wretchedly politicized, spending her influence on acquiring wealth. From the start I must insist we observe the biblical distinction, though it is not apparent to the human eye, between the church as the body of all who truly belong to Christ and those human institutions that carry his name (whether deserving or not).

If I am now in a position to defend the Roman Catholic Inquisition, of all things, it's stranger to me than I can say. Such a thing is more horrifying in my eyes than it can even be in yours—to say nothing of how it appears in God's eyes.

Yet though the case can be overstated, it is true enough that people who identify themselves with Christ, who act without so much as a word of justification from the Christian Scriptures, do awful things. Sadder still is the fact that even people who do hold sincere faith in Christ can nevertheless be tragically misguided. Yes, even true Christians can be tempted to surrender in miserable weakness to the very worst inclinations of fallen human nature. To deny this would not be to support orthodox Christian theology but actually to argue against it. Members of Christ's church have at times picked up the sword and made it bloody.

People say, "If that's what it means to believe in God, I don't want any part of it!" They simplistically assume that all religion is cut from one cloth, even though the founder of Islam died saying, "Death to all Christians. Death to all Jews," and the object of my faith died saying, "Father, forgive them." I take no pleasure in pointing this out, believe me. But it is the real sayings of Muhammad and the real teachings of Islam and its Qur'an that make it difficult for Muslims to issue a convincing protest against the violence being perpetrated in our world by worshipers of Allah. If anyone dares to act violently in the name of Jesus, not only is the violence against him, but the notion is so offensive and absurd that every credible spokesperson for Christianity unites in a loud outcry. Why do they do this? The answer is standing there at the entrance of the Garden of Gethsemane.

"Put your sword away."

What that moment makes so clear is that when the visible church handles worldly weapons and worldly power, she plainly leaves the path her founder laid down. Fifth-century bishop Augustine put it so succinctly, "No philosophy can properly be judged by its abuse." Jesus has been misrepresented, betrayed, and, yes, abused by those who claim to follow him, as he himself predicted. It is as simple as that. Whether you have in mind the witch hunters from five centuries ago or pedophile priests in this one, it is no surprise in such a world as this that the very worst sorts of people will claim to be the champions of Christ—some nefariously, some with honest but horribly misguided intentions. Rest assured that nothing you can say about such people is more horrifying to contemplate than what the Lord himself will say if they do not repent.

"I never knew you. Away from me."[126]

In a way it is understandable that the church is disparaged for failings that often are far more prevalent among irreligious people. We, as members of the church, mean to follow Christ and can only accept criticism for the times we do not deserve our association with him. However, there is a significant point to be made by comparing the Christian church at her worst, on the one hand, with the evil and violence done in the name of atheism, on the other. In the latter case there has been no abandoning of the espoused position, but rather, the philosophy has been carried to its logical conclusion. It is easily demonstrated that evil done in the name of Christ is, in truth, the ultimate abandonment of Christ. However, if someone who says that there is no God and, therefore, no ultimate morality, should commit the same evil act, it is not a betrayal of his or her philosophy but its ultimate expression. Do you see the difference?

Now I am not saying that all atheists are violent killers, not at all. The atheists I've known have been very pleasant people trying to live decent lives, that is to say, they live above their own philosophy. Their unbelief is not providing the reasons for them to live as they do. Please don't try to say, "No one kills in the name of atheism," for what else is it when a man snuffs out a life because "he felt like it"? The dirty little secret of atheism, acknowledged by Frederick Nietzsche, Charles Darwin, and the rest, is that there remains a logical, reasonable (and ice cold) path that leads directly from the atheistic philosophy to all the blood that has flowed wherever atheism has been the reigning ideology. Think of Nazi Germany, Communist China, and Communist Russia, for starters. The enthusiasm with which a young Adolf Hitler studied the philosophical ravings of Nietzsche has been well documented. Holocaust survivor Victor Frankl observed that the tortures he witnessed and endured were not invented by mad warmongers in Berlin but rather "at the desks and in the well-lit lecture halls of nihilistic scientists and philosophers."[127]

These words of Hitler are on display in a gas chamber in Auschwitz above a pile of women's hair: "I freed Germany from the stupid and degrading fallacies of conscience and morality."[128]

The tenet that there is no God—and, therefore, no right or wrong written largely across our world—cannot provide a single compelling reason for a man not to do whatever comes into his heart to do. From Jesus, and only from Jesus, comes the very good reason to gladly surrender your life in self-sacrificing love. He did it first for us.

I submit that we need more, not less, of that true religion that compels all people to examine their own hearts, to be reduced to sorrow over what they see, and to see in Christ what only Christianity clearly sees . . . that "God is love."[129] And not only is he the love that always forgives and always heals, but he is the love that always compels.

"Love your enemies."[130]

"Do good to those who hate you."[131]

"Bless and do not curse."[132]

Ravi Zecharias, a Christian (Evangelical) author, has pointed out that you can't name a place on earth today where people because of their faith are in danger for their lives at the hands of Christians. Not a single one. Although religions nonsensically lumped together make a convenient target, it is naïve to suggest that otherwise good people are corrupted by religion to do evil things that otherwise would not have occurred to them. If falsified religion were not the mantle under which men cloak their right to hurt and to kill and to steal to have whatever they want and to act out their historical grudges, it would be something else. In fact, let's take this challenge—that the church has done some horrible things—and turn it completely upside down. The fact that people could be so violent and hateful in Jesus' name, in spite of who he is and what he has done, says nothing about Jesus. It does speak volumes about the condition of the human heart. So this very objection points to the principle blind spot of atheism—what humanistic philosophy has been completely unwilling to see—namely, what humanity is really like.

As I write my nation is reeling from the terrorist attacks on the United States. If we were willing to see the truth buried with the body parts under the rubble of the World Trade Center, we might ask, "What in the world could ever atone for this human race?"

We can only think back to that night when hundreds of men fell backward at the sound of God speaking his own name . . . and still Jesus went with them. Recall the stunning willingness with which the great "I AM" surrendered himself to the worst that men could do. He loves us—all of us—and gave his life up for us. The one who lives to plead for us in heaven would indeed have us fight for him. But how?

When we within the church turn on the world with even so much as arrogant disgust, hypocritical outrage, or gleeful condemnation, the one we say we're following still cries, "Put your sword away!" The weapon we wield when our eyes are on him, when we're in him, is his powerful Word of grace. "For God did not send his Son into the world to condemn the world, but to save the world through him."[133]

I only pray that you are prepared to read the real lesson chiseled into Christian church history, namely, just how powerful the Christian message is. Christianity has seemingly died many times over. For example, it rose with the Roman Empire to wrap its arms around the world, and when that empire fell, it should have been the end of this faith as well. Yet when Christianity dies, it is always unstoppably reborn, essentially unchanged, in another time, in another land. After all, Chesterton observed, Christianity's founder "knew his way out of a grave."[134]

Name another belief that has so transcended every barrier of culture, race, and time or that has survived unchanged at its essence for so many thousands of years. It is on the power of the outrageous promise of Christ, when only 12 stood close enough to hear it—"I will build my church, and the gates of Hades will not overcome it"[135]— that the greatest tide in human history has lapped also at my shore. I do not refer to the human institutions of visible Christianity but to the true church, the body of all those dear ones spread across time who actually knew him. As a gracious gathering of flawed people, the church on earth is deeply flawed. But you see, I learn about Jesus from her. And yes, I love her.

Please bear in mind that history has not only recorded the church's failures and the dismal betrayal of Christ by those who never knew him at all. History also has witnessed that the people of the world sometimes sit back to wonder at the people of God—how they love one another, pray for their enemies, follow Jesus.

"They spare nothing," observed the ancient pagan Lucian about the compassion of ancient believers.

"(Jesus) has put it into their heads that they are all brothers."[136]

Indeed, the church has done beautiful things.

You have car trouble and are stranded in a crime-infested neighborhood. It's night. Six bulky men stream out of a house and make their way toward you. Now, be honest, would it make any difference to you at all to know that the house they just left is where they hold their weekly Bible study?

Saying yes is your admission that the influence of Christ, by his Word, is a good one after all. His Spirit is one that tugs toward love and self-forgetting. His is an impulse to gladly serve, to gladly die, and to let the world discover that the safest place on earth is among the twos and threes that gather in his name.

For there he is.

"Jesus never claimed to be God"

After Moses had spent 40 anonymous years in a land of strangers, it was time. God came near. He drew the 80-year-old man toward a strange, unearthly light up on the side of a mountain. There Moses sank to his knees before a bush that burned and burned, trying to comprehend what the Voice was telling him.

"Take off your sandals, Moses, the ground you are walking on is holy ground. . . . I've seen the misery of my people. I've heard them crying. So I have come down to rescue them."

"B-b-but when they ask me your name, what will I tell them?"

A simple question. And the name of the Voice?

"I AM."

That magnificent, true story was 1,500 years old when a young man, whose name means "rescue," stood before a weary, threatening court. They asked Jesus a simple question, "Are you the Son of the Blessed One?" When he answered, the ripping of the high priest's robe meant that he was understood all too well.

"I AM."[137]

It may have been those two words, more than any others, that began the beating that would continue throughout the night . . . until beating him wasn't enough. Just two words, but the glow of the burning bush hung all about them. These two words whispered, "Take off your shoes," because if they were true, then the very ground was holy again. And the people who venerated Moses were meeting the One who made Moses, the One who saw the misery of his people, who heard them crying . . .

And came down.

(Please read Mark 14:53-65.)

You hear this objection every now and then: "Jesus never claimed to be God. It's what other people said about him." In another chapter I addressed the authenticity of the four gospels. Taking those accounts at face value as we have every reason to do, I want to tell you about just one of the many times Jesus was breathtakingly clear.

The shortest complete sentence in the English language— I am—represents the greatest claim any human being has ever made for himself. To catch Jesus' meaning, it helps to understand the historical context as described in the story above. I AM is the name of the Lord as revealed to Moses at a time when his own dear people were living the withering life of slavery. The name I AM pulses with God's own unchanging reality and absolute self-sufficiency. This was God's marvelous self-expression dawning on a lost, suffering, skeptical land. His name was the single thing they most desperately needed to know, the answer to their truest questions.

"God, are you who they say you are? Are you watching us, remembering us and all the promises you made? Are you somewhere listening to our crying, somehow crying along with us? Are you on your way to deliver us and bring us home . . . or . . . are you even there?"

"I AM."

Yes, God has a name. Now you can begin to understand how those two words sounded as they left the lips of Jesus to echo off the walls of that chamber and why the people reacted as they did. The question on the floor was, "Are you the Son of the Blessed One?" If you have any doubt of Jesus' meaning in answering, "I AM," you need only peel your eyes off him and watch the people of his own culture, time, and place react to him. In this particular story, it's the ripping of the high priest's robe and the shocked cry of "blasphemy" that confirm what the good rabbi was saying.

In other accounts what profoundly disturbed so many was the way Jesus spoke about God as no one else ever had. He would refer to him simply as "my Father." It was always "my Father's will" and "my Father's house," always this startling note of familiarity and of something more. The people who heard him through distinctively Jewish ears cried, "[He makes] himself equal with God."[138] Equality with God! My point? When it comes to these expressions always rolling off the tongue of Christ—"my Father" and "I AM"—we can trust his contemporaries to know precisely what he meant by them, even when modern scholarship pretends not to.

Now while some were shocked, I must quickly add that there were others, thousands of them, who were shocked at first . . . and then believed. The convinced included Jesus' own mother, brothers, and members of the Jewish Sanhedrin. Please remember that these people were not pagans predisposed to the thought of "gods" (and curiously human ones at that) making nuisances of themselves in the world of women and men. No, these were the children of Abraham, with faith fueled by holy fear. These were people who dared not speak the name of the "Wholly Other," that invisible, transcendent God, the One who carved the mountains and formed the seas with the raw power of his Word. With their unique conception of God—the very highest one possible—it is inconceivable that they should call some man God just because they loved him. The notion that these people, of all people, conveyed this status on Jesus out of their own misguided loyalty and affection is clearly absurd. This is the very last place on earth you would expect such a movement, founded on the faith that a cruci-fied man was the Lord of glory himself, to erupt with the explosive force that it did.

I want you to take in the staggering historical fact that among the very ones who gave to the world the true con-cept of God as a wholly transcendent, ineffable, and infi-nite deity there arose this stubborn faith in a man carrying a cross. They were weaned on the story of the pillar of fire that led their fathers out of slavery to a mountain that shook with the glory of God. . . . And they became con-vinced that this teacher was that very God. They recog-nized that it was Jesus who sent all the prophets of the Old Testament,[139] that it is Jesus who holds the right to forgive human sin,[140] that it is Jesus who is the ultimate source of spiritual life,[141] that it is Jesus who is the ultimate judge pre-siding over the life of every human being.[142]

In fact, consider that last point. Jesus taught his follow-ers to find the source of all human depravities within them-selves and to be broken before God in repentance. There was no other way to approach the Father in heaven. Indeed, people who come closest to God are the most aware of their own desperate need for his mercy and forgiveness. Paradoxically, Jesus himself, whose moral standard included perfect love for his bitterest enemies, never felt any need to repent. Not ever. His self-awareness was free of even the slightest taint of shame.[143] It's yet another way the implicit claim of divinity was not only made by Jesus but consis-tently lived by him.

The truth is, no one put the words into his mouth. This is all Jesus:

"While I am in the world, I am the light of the world."[144]

"I am the way and the truth and the life."[145]

"Before Abraham was born, I am!"[146]

John Stott puts it succinctly in his book *Basic Christianity*. He states that according to Jesus, "to know him was to know God,[147] to see him was to see God,[148] to believe in him was to believe in God,[149] to receive him was to receive God,[150] to hate him was to hate God,[151] and to honor him was to honor God."[152]

We must be clear. This is the central claim. This is what Christians believe. It remains the centerpiece of the magnificent, true story that can be understood in no other way.

This man claimed to be the Son of God.

It never occurred to Buddha or Confucius. Muhammad didn't dare. Only Jesus makes himself the focal point of his teaching. Only Jesus could make the utterly convincing claim of personal moral perfection with no fear of contradiction. Only Jesus claims deity and sets himself utterly apart.

That is so clear that we are left to wonder where such a notion comes from that Jesus never claimed to be God. Coming from academics familiar with history and its validations, frankly, it seems disingenuous. Did you read Mark chapter 14? When you got to the part where scholars tried to come up with some charge, any charge, against Jesus, did it occur to you that you are still being lied to by people who have their own private reasons for wishing he would go away?

G. K. Chesterton observed that when it comes to beating Jesus, it seems any stick will do.[153] Why is that? What makes people accept unquestioningly and then repeat as fact virtually any excuse to dismiss the claims of Jesus? Perhaps there's a simple answer. To hear the claims of Jesus Christ is to suddenly know that it is, in fact, he who has a judgment to make about us. Modern skepticism puts God himself—the God of all goodness, of all life, of all love—in the defendant's chair, absurdly wondering not whether we can possibly be vindicated but if he can. But make no mistake. He is not on trial. Not anymore. It is we poor sinners that await the word from him—the up-or-down verdict on our very lives. For many, that is reason enough to find some charge, any charge, against him . . . and reach for the blindfold of Mark chapter 14 . . . and tighten their fists. Thus they fail to hear or to grasp what God's judgment, which he has entrusted to his only Son, actually is.

"I forgive you."

To be very clear, I am not trying to construct a logically ironclad case for Jesus but one that ultimately rests on the Word of Jesus himself. The reason lies in the very nature of the question of faith. In the end it's not a rational conclusion about a set of facts that is called for. There stands a person. He offers a relationship. He makes extravagant promises about what is in God's heart toward you on the basis of what he himself has accomplished.

"I am returning to my Father and your Father."[154]

"I am going there to prepare a place for you."[155]

"I am."

Such promises stand outside the realm of proofs and arguments. They are meant for you to believe.

As the first nail is driven in and blood soaks into the ground, he cries, "Father . . ."

There he goes again.

"Father, forgive them."

Some tear their clothes. Some fall to their knees.

Peter moves toward the fire to try to keep warm. In the quiet security of his circle of friends, it was easy to say "What I would do if . . ." and to believe himself. All that seems a million miles away now. Jesus was arrested, and Peter ran away with the others.

Now, trying to blend in with a faceless crowd, he has "Galilean" written all over him.

"Say, weren't you with Jesus?"

"You were, weren't you?"

"Yes, I'm almost sure of it!"

With familiar old curses, Peter strains to convince them he does not know the man. It seems to work. If he looked like one of the followers of Jesus before, he does not anymore.

The rooster crows again. Oh, Lord. Again!

Inside the chambers of the high priest, if they notice it at all amid the shouting, they certainly don't understand why the silent Jesus turns his head. He meets Peter's eyes for one unbearable moment, then turns back to what he is doing, back to dying.

Peter cries and cries. Over Jesus. Over himself.

Friends, these are important tears. We don't read that Judas cried or, for that matter, Pontius Pilate. It's that desperate weeping outside the high priest's court that we always come back to—when

Peter has just plain had it with Peter. Judging from the rest of his story, one that will come to display the very meanings of loyalty and selfless courage, one thing is clear.

It is a good cry.

His tears aren't doing him any harm.

(Please read Luke 22:54-62.)

"I confess that I am by nature sinful . . . for this I deserve your punishment both now and in eternity." As jarring as the Sunday morning words sound, remain on the outside of that confession and this entire Christian faith remains a closed book. So I have to ask, is this the real reason you deny the existence of a moral lawgiver (God) and the old absolutes (right and wrong)?

You want to "feel good about yourself"?

While I acknowledge the anguish of a poor self-image, I question the fundamental premises of the self-esteem movement. Is it so absurd to suggest that these feelings of self-loathing are not the problem itself, only the symptoms of something even worse? Is not the painful thinking so common to the human experience—"It is killing me that I am not what I'm supposed to be"—the relentless expression of something objectively true? We don't merely feel unacceptable. We actually are.

There is something really wrong with us, and the knowledge of it hurts.

A hint of that something wrong is found in the fact that, before sin, Adam apparently didn't notice he was naked. Our first father, newly fallen, was asked by God, "Who told you that you were naked?"[156] Can you imagine? Before this Adam must have been a man utterly, blissfully lost in the worship of his God and the wonder of his world and Eve his wife that God should come wondering how Adam had come to reflect on himself at all. It's staggering to realize how far Adam fell from that innocent unself-conscious joy, with us hidden, as it were, in his body.

Consider the implications of the fact that we were designed for relationships with God and people. It means that we were not at all designed to meet our own need for love. The gravitational pull of my self—the way I manage to make everything in my world end up being about my needs, my wants, and my feelings—is the very opposite of love. This is the dry and dusty sign of our spiritual deadness. As Don Matzat has written, it's not *what* I think of myself, but *that* I do—irresistibly, without fail—that is the source of my spiritual misery.[157] That is why the obsession with loving ourselves will never turn into a deeper capacity to love anyone else, only a deeper and deadlier fascination with ourselves. As sinners we can never be the source of our own healing and life.

Is the concept so hard to grasp? We need God. Though we don't deserve him, we will groan in empty, restless misery until we have him.

I've told the story of Peter, as psychologically rich a portrayal as any in the Bible, to bring this discussion back to real life. Is it not appropriate to be sorry for what we are? The deceptively simple question is this, Does Peter have something to cry about or not? You saw what he did—should he or should he not be weeping? The painfully obvious truth is that Peter has his reasons to be sorry, just as I have mine and you have yours.

My purpose is not to make you cry and cry as he did. The degree of emotion that accompanies your repentance is not the point. More vital is that certain knowledge that if we only once saw all things as they are, we would be undone by guilt and shame . . . as Peter was. Peter saw his offense not merely in relation to a moral code but in relation to a person who had only been good to him. Peter saw the truth many people successfully avoid for years, that what he had said and had done revealed what he was. He may have protested, "I'm not the sort of man that runs out on a friend." Clearly he was. Whether such knowledge drives us into the dark to weep or to another drink or to another stupid argument or to another hour of overtime to prove that we're worthwhile, the only way out of this darkness is through it.

What matters most is that we give up already, that we concur with the judgment God has made about us. He declares us sinners worthy of eternal death. He will use his Word, our own consciences, and to some degree the circumstances of our lives to persuade us to agree. This is not to hurt us. This is God drawing near.

"I live in a high and holy place, but also with him who is contrite and lowly in spirit."[158]

So I call myself a sinner worthy of death though it feels like death and find that it is on this hinge that the door of Christianity swings open. "But I love you," Someone says and lifts my downcast eyes. "Come and see how much." It is God come near in the dying and rising Christ.

It remains a defining truth in every Christian life: We must see our sins if we are to see our Savior. If you would just once witness the crucifixion of Christ through the tears of Peter, you would know what the Scriptures call "godly sorrow . . . that . . . leaves no regret."[159] How hungry are you for that? While the world fears the psychological damage of calling ourselves sinners, the real harm is done when guilt, unacknowledged and unresolved, is left to poison a life. God's Word speaks of repentance by which we are "not harmed in any way."[160] Another says, "Repent . . . that times of refreshing may may come."[161] Refreshing! Words are too weak to express how my spirit freshly soars on the other side of my tears. I know this, that no one can condemn me—no one in this world, no one outside of it, not anymore. No one can condemn me . . . for I condemn myself . . . and God, my God, rushes to my defense.

"Be of good cheer, your sins are forgiven."[162]

Seeing always more of myself that I may always see more of Christ: this is repentance. It is a gift only God can give.[163] It is a way of life. I recognize personal idolatries behind all my personal anxieties, selfishness fueling my sadness, and the ways I am bad looming larger in my mind than the ways I've been hurt. But he still did what he did. I am willing to taste Peter's sorrow that I may also know his "inexpressible and glorious joy,"[164] for out of the soil of confession—not embracing the self but putting it to death—there arises a life that is free, finally free, and a new thing in Christ.

This is the essence of a relationship with God, its beginning and its end: In Christ God calls us forgiven . . . and we believe him. And the life that is in Jesus—the love, the peace, the joy, the hope—comes to us when our minds are fixed on him.

Is there no proper place for loving ourselves? I wonder. If I could only learn from Christ Jesus to love all people—just because they are people, just because they are loved by him—then I would accept myself and could live with myself in that same detached, grace-filled way. It is probably better not to think of ourselves at all. So we "fix our eyes on Jesus,"[165] as the Scriptures invite us. Through his own Spirit, a deeper, truer thirst than that of "feeling good about ourselves" is making itself known.

"I want to know Christ."[166]

As C. S. Lewis wrote, "Look for yourself, and you will find in the long run only hatred, loneliness, despair, rage, ruin and decay. But look for Christ and you will find him, and with him everything else thrown in."[167]

Have no fear of what Christians call repentance. It is a good cry.

When my daughter can still say, from the heart, that she is sorry, I know that her heart is still mine. It's how I know there is hope for a marriage, for a friendship, for a church—our sins sometimes break our hearts.

But there stands Jesus, his face turned toward us.

"There's no such thing as truth"

A governor of this world and the Prince of the other met face to face—Pontius Pilate and Jesus Christ. The dialogue in that Friday morning light was so fascinating you could almost forget that one held the life of the other in his hands.

Jesus said, "For this reason I was born, and for this I came into the world, to testify to the truth. Everyone on the side of truth listens to me."

Did you hear that? "Pilate, if you were on the side of truth you would be listening to me. Ultimate Truth, brilliant and unavoidable, is standing directly in front of you. The question is, Do you really want to know?"

You see, knowing the truth about this particular case would have been dreadfully inconvenient. Given what Pilate had to do to Jesus (because of his own political problems), it was much easier to stay confused. He willfully closed his eyes.

"What is truth?" Pilate muttered as he turned away, stepping out of the light as quickly as he could. For when clear and simple truth no longer rules the day, when any version of truth is as good as any other, then it is blind power that rules the day instead. Vicious, brute, crucifying power.

While every achievement of Pontius Pilate is forgotten, this single conversation, this brief moment in broad daylight, lasts and lasts. Millions recite his name, remembering this one thing only—Truth itself was once "crucified under Pontius Pilate."

And that Truth, having been murdered, rose again.

(Please read John 18:28-40.)

Ravi Zecharias remembers touring the Wexner Center for the Arts at Ohio State University. With beams going everywhere, stairways leading nowhere, and columns that don't actually meet the floor, the structure is designed to reflect life itself, "senseless and incoherent." It invites those who enter to question everything, especially the old absolutes, the worn-out truths that simple people once took for granted. But a plainspoken tourist asked the painfully obvious question, "Did they do the same thing with the foundation?" And the whole statement of the designers was undone.

Those who designed that building actually knew full well that there are certain undeniables—principles that don't change and those that cannot be violated without serious consequence.[168] They knew it. Why don't we?

According to one survey, 67 percent of Americans say they don't believe there is any such thing as truth. Should a Christian testimony intrude on a television talk show or in a secular classroom, the sophisticated thing is to dismiss it this way: "That may be true for you; that doesn't mean it's true for everyone." I have to ask whether they've thought that dismissal through.

A young man fresh from Philosophy 101 at a secular university informed me with undisguised condescension that "one must never make a statement that means to negate other points of view." This is how he meant to negate mine. Some people argue with dogmatic certainty against the very possibility of dogmatic certainty. Many will confidently insist that everybody can be right in their private version of "truth," citing this as the reason Christians cannot be. There is a breathtaking claim that goes like this: "Anyone who says that others are wrong in their own personal truth is simply intolerant." The next question is painfully obvious. But . . . isn't that precisely what you are saying to me?

"It's impossible to know anything!"

"And you know this . . . how?"

Enough. The truth is that we live our lives every day—we cross busy streets and sit on chairs—as if reality can be known. Not exhaustively perhaps, but well enough. Is it not the ultimate in self-defeating philosophies when people look you in the eye and say, "There is no truth," really believing that they're saying something true! If they're right, they're wrong. Such notions don't need to be refuted. They refute themselves.

Is there no reality that exists "out there," apart from our thoughts about it? You can't think of anything that would stand as true even if the whole world called it false? Does reality really twist and change to conform to what each person happens to think at the time? No such thing as truth? I realize that to speak this way is the cost of admission in our sophisticated circles of higher learning. In the view of journalist Malcolm Muggeridge, "We have educated ourselves into imbecility."

If relativism makes sense to you, it is likely that you are, as popular theologian Francis Schaeffer put it, "living below the level of despair." In *The God Who Is There*, he writes of the seismic changes in human thought dating back to the early years of the last century and articulates the very real despair of all those "enlightened ones" who deny truth and abandon all hope that there is any cohesive answer to life. What are they really saying, those who say, "There is no truth"?

First of all, growing numbers of people are fuzzy on what is called the law of non-contradiction. The law of non-contradiction states, "If A is true, then non-A is false." In other words, something cannot be both true and false at the same time and in the same way. Closely related is the concept of antithesis, which is the way any statement negates its true opposite. As Schaeffer wrote, a person cannot even communicate with himself, much less with anyone else, except on the basis of antithesis. If I think to myself, "That blossom is beautiful," I really mean to contradict the opposite of those words . . . unless we plan to give up on words and thinking altogether. (By the way, if you try to argue *against* the law of non-contradiction or if you do try to speak without antithesis, hopefully the irony of your position will suddenly occur to you. Think about it.)

These are the things, as self-evident as they are, that you must ignore if you want to hold to relativism, if you want to keep insisting that contradictory statements can be equally valid and that each person can legitimately hold his or her own version of truth. Now it is well and good to say that because each person looks at the world from his or her own unique point of view, it is *as if* each person lives in a different world and it is *like* having individual realities. It is nonsense to suggest that reality actually is different for each person and that opposite statements can be equally valid in describing reality. The denial of absolute truth is based on an absurdity and is the seed of existential despair. My sincere prayer is that people would take the meaninglessness of this thinking (and of the life that grows out it) for what it is. This meaninglessness is a sign of their alienation from my God.

His name in Hebrew is *Elohim-Amen*, "the God of truth."[169]

He knows all. He sees all. He is the One who is able to name reality as it actually is, to describe himself as he is, and us as we are. The truth he reveals by his Word is not exhaustive, but it is knowable. Knowledge by God's revelation is more empirical and less circular than any other way of knowing—logic is supportable only by more logic, intuition by more intuition, and so on and so on. Only God cannot lie. And shutting your ears to his Word simply doesn't make sense.

I think I understand, however, what makes people hold on to the notion of relativism without completely thinking it through to the ruddy end. They think they're being kind. They think life is like a piece of modern art, all squiggles and blotches. All that's really there is chaos, so every attempt to find meaning on that canvas is only someone acting out his or her strange need to impose "truth" where none actually exists. So, as their thinking goes, the kind and generous thing is to let each passerby offer his or her own opinion about what it means. No one can claim perfect objectivity, so we will call each interpretation as good as every other. But I submit that when people begin to look at all things—at life and the human soul, at religion and morality, at family and sexuality and little unborn people—as if they are vague abstractions, the results are anything but kind. Take the man who pathetically murmurs, "Whatever"—that distinctively modern version of "What is truth?"—when his greed or unfaithfulness or violence is plainly without excuse.

The loving thing is to warn you that we dare not play this kind of game with God. "Without excuse" is the simple verdict he passes on those who deny what they already know.[170] The problem is not lack of evidence for the truth, but the hypocrisy of those who claim to be searching for it. People "suppress the truth"[171]—that is what is really going on. Why? They are deeply hostile to the thought of anything that in any sense stands in judgment on them,[172] much less finds them wanting. In the plainspoken insight of Jesus, "Everyone who does evil hates the light, and will not come into the light for fear that his deeds will be exposed."[173] The old absolutes, if allowed to stand, lay waste to all such rationalizations. So people willfully close their minds to the dazzling design of creation, to the persistent nagging of conscience, to the integrity of biblical revelation, and most of all to Jesus.

You may be wondering if I really question the fact that each person looks at life through a unique human lens, shaped by culture and experience. Actually, I agree that finding ultimate truth is impossible, that is, for us. However, this begs the real question: Cannot God reveal truth? Cannot light shine in from the outside? Today's relativism has nothing important to say about the possibility of divine revelation. Cannot God, who exists beyond the reaches of reason, make himself knowable and known?

After all, if God were simply to reveal Truth, what would his Truth be like? It would include such things as "no mind has conceived."[174] That is, no matter how simple the message might be, it would still be thoroughly counterintuitive, defying the centuries of human guesswork. People would certainly resist it and would do so with disdain. But not all would successfully resist. Those who would receive this revealed truth would only describe it, well, the way they would describe Jesus.

"A light shining in a dark place."[175]

Lastly, if ultimate truth can only be found if it intrudes on the epistemological confusion (the impossibility of finding ultimate truth by ourselves), then real truth would need to be apprehended in a unique way, set apart from any other.

"Trust in God," spoke the Light. "Trust also in me."[176]

We have been living all this time within a work of art, a creation, a masterpiece. See the order, the beauty, the intelligence, the kindness. Then one day at Bethlehem, the Artist himself stepped in through a door the size of a birth canal. Examine his words to Pilate. This was not only a birth; it was also a "coming" by the one who would tell us precisely what it all means. No more scratching our heads. No more insisting that a question mark hangs over everyone and everything. Jesus came in from outside of human bewilderment. He came to be the Truth—to become the perfect revelation of exactly who God is, what his work means, what he thinks of you, what he intends for you, what is in his heart and mind toward you. Yes, we are without excuse for all of our sins. That's the truth.

But so is this: Jesus stood there holding Pilate's life in his own hands . . . and mine . . . and everyone's. Only open your eyes. Watch Jesus reach with brilliant, self-evident words for his own murderer, for Pontius Pilate, as for one more last-second disciple.

"Everyone on the side of truth listens to me."

By his Spirit, his words have taken captive my soul. The truth is that he was reaching for us all when he reached for the cross, gripping it like a prize.

I know that there is love beyond all telling at the center of all things. Holding all things together is such a One who would stand there, kneel there, hang there . . . for me. I will step into that light one day and stand in that love. It will wash over me and in me and through me. I will meet Truth face to face.

What I know for sure is . . . Jesus.

When I stand at the door of eternity, there is only one face I'll be looking for, only one Savior who can speak certainty into my death.

"I tell you the truth, today you will be with me in paradise."[177]

Stand with me. Reclaim your longing to know one thing that's real and to find one place where you can stand that will remain forever solid beneath your feet.

"I tell you the truth."

"Do last-minute confessions get people into heaven?"

Lifted up half naked, the punch line of merciless jokes, Jesus achieved a death of dignity and grace that hardly seems possible. Other men faced crucifixion with curses and cringing. They groveled and wept. This one prayed.

"Father, forgive them, for they do not know what they are doing."

It takes your breath away. Any eyes that were open were drawn to the sign over his head, Jesus of Nazareth, King of the Jews.

This one is a King.

Nearby, crucified with Christ, was just another nameless thief, just another forgettable criminal who broke some mother's heart. Yet if that's all you see, look again. As far as the gospels record, he was the only one at the crucifixion of Christ who spoke a word in Jesus' defense. And he was the only one who said a single kind thing to the lonely Jesus as he was dying. One more distinction that first startles and then makes perfect sense: he is the only one in all of the Scriptures to do something I've been doing all my life. He addressed Jesus as simply "Jesus," with no other accompanying title.

"Jesus, remember me when you come into your kingdom."

Think of these two men whittled down to their essences. A nameless thief and just plain Jesus. One is guilt personified, the other, love. The criminal deserves nothing other than death—he says so himself—so he makes no claim. He asks only to be a memory in the heart of his dying God. He only wants to say, "I believe you, Jesus. I know a King when I see one."

"I tell you the truth," Jesus said, "today you will be with me in paradise."

(Please read Luke 23:32-43.)

"Do I have this straight? People can cause misery their entire lives, call out his name with their last breath, hear some Christian absolve them in Jesus' name, and wake up in heaven? That's it? Just like that?" It's a good question. Does the proverbial killer on death row get to make a last-minute confession as the door is closing and enter paradise? The answer is even better.

Yes.

The question is too important for me to evade, soft-pedal, or otherwise offer a more palatable answer than Jesus gave this dying thief: "I tell you the truth, today you will be with me in paradise!"

The question is too important, first, because it confronts us with what the Christian faith actually is. "For God so loved the world that he gave his one and only Son, that whoever believes in him shall not perish but have eternal life."[178] It's as simple as this: *whoever* means *whoever.*

World means *world.*

Understand that my answer to the problem of the deathbed confession does not minimize in any way the misery a person leaves behind. I'm not asking you to look past the awful things people have done with their lives as if inconsequential. In fact, if murderers, for example, have genuinely received God's forgiveness before dying, you can know that they were made to see themselves and what they did and to have their taste of sorrow. Without true repentance, the conversion fools no one, least of all God.

However, the solution to the dilemma of thieves and killers landing safely in heaven lies in another place entirely. Their crimes are great, awful mountains of guilt that grew with every passing day. All I'm saying is that there is something else greater still. I point to the enormity of the gift that God gave.

"Where sin increased, grace increased all the more."[179]

This is the question to be asked and answered: If God has given his one and only Son, is this enough to atone for this entire world, or is it not? Christians are the ones shouting "Yes!" and "Glory!" The sacrifice of God the Son is enough to atone for ten thousand worlds if that were necessary. Go to the cross, and open your eyes. Rest assured that no human crime went unpunished, yet by the sacrifice of Christ we sinners are declared innocent for his sake alone, purely by grace. I ask you, Is this cause for complaint or undying praise?

People like to put this objection in what seem to be the crassest terms possible. Could Adolf Hitler have gone to heaven if he had repented on his deathbed . . . and would he have passed Mother Theresa on her way to hell if she had not? While the premise is absurd, the answer, theoretically at least, is yes on both accounts. And though it may seem like a wrinkle in Christian theology that admits bad people to heaven ahead of people seemingly better by far, the Bible can rather easily clarify. According to the Word of God, everyone is a sinner after all. Everyone. Both Hitler and Mother Theresa were steeped in sin (and she would have told you the same thing, quite convincingly I might add). And although the symptoms of this fatal disease do vary greatly from case to case, everyone will die from it. "The wages of sin is death."[180] The remarkable thing is not the apparent goodness or badness of souls in heaven or hell. The gift, the miracle, the wonder is that anyone ultimately survives his or her own sin to stand in the joy of him forever. Such glory is possible for no one left to himself or herself and for everyone by the sheer grace of God.

I observe that this objection, which starts out rather theoretical and academic (and in a way self-righteous), has a way of becoming something else entirely. Another reason I must give such a clear answer is for the day when the question becomes my own. Should I harm a child, for example, I know what should happen to me, though I would prefer a millstone around my neck. Some day the full weight of the harder Scriptures dealing with lust and anger, envy and pride, may wrap around your soul. One day God may show you *you*. You'll be "sinking down, sinking down beneath God's righteous frown . . ." and the question suddenly will not be theoretical or academic but dreadfully personal. "How far does grace extend? Is it too late for me? Can a person go beyond the reach of grace?"

"Have I?"

I speak from experience. Although on Sundays I confess that "I am altogether sinful from birth" and that I "deserve only God's wrath," there is in me a stubborn determination to resist that very knowledge. It feels like self-preservation. I don't want to see to the bottom of those truths. Instead, during the week I find I am hungry to know just the opposite of what I've confessed. I daily enter my world searching for the evidence that I am actually a pretty good guy doing well. And although, to the observer, my life seems to "work," don't let me fool you. Sometimes I cannot resist the awful knowledge that God is entirely right about me. His verdict on my life, that it has been wrong from the start, is true. I am just another thief, facing my mortality, crying out the obvious about the long shadow of death in this world, "I am getting what my deeds deserve." I take my place among the murderers and silently slip in among the thieves. I am nothing but a worthless sinner fit to be utterly condemned, a criminal to be gotten rid of with nails if necessary. That's what God's Word says, and in moments of brutal clarity, I pass the same sentence on myself.

That's when I die.

I am crucified, and I die with Christ.

I see it now. There was nothing for God to do with me but condemn me. That's exactly what he did, except that he substituted his Son. I see that awful death of Jesus and know that it was mine. It didn't happen to me, but it should have. And in coming to that dreadful conclusion about myself, the identification with him is complete. I am crucified with Christ.

This is the death that frees me.

For since I am "united with him like this in his death,"[181] then I am united with him in that tomb when his still chest suddenly heaved in a breath and he was alive again from the dead. Through the forgiveness of all my sin, I arise a new thing in Jesus my Lord, and all because he remembered me. I turn away from my sinful self, from all my serious concern about myself, as from a dead thing. When my eyes are on Jesus, just Jesus, I take hold of the life that really is life. "I have been crucified with Christ and I no longer live, but Christ lives in me. The life I live in the body, I live by faith in the Son of God, who loved me and gave himself for me."[182]

When it comes to eternal life in the presence of my God, the gates of paradise stand open. I am already let in. A forgiven man, alive to God, I see one more reason the question of this chapter is so critical.

Someday, someone will need grace from me.

He was a good talker who conned me out of 80 dollars that were no doubt spent on drugs. That was during my first year of ministry. Only God himself could have brought me together with this same man eight years later . . . when the drugs had nearly finished their work. At the age of 45, he was nearly dead. The only response he could make as I read the Scriptures to him week after week was to close his eyes when we prayed and once or twice squeeze out a tear. I and my dying thief.

At a time like that there is only the Word of Christ—there is nothing more. There is only the holy pleasure of sitting in a dimly lit room with the shadow of death all around with this as the only light.

"I tell you the truth, today you will be with me in paradise."

I know how far the grace of God extends.

I've learned that *world* means *world*.

"The Christian faith is too negative"

A secret disciple from the ranks of Jewish leadership, Nicodemus stepped out of the shadows to ask for the body of Christ. At great personal cost, he and another Pharisee, Joseph of Arimathea, climbed that dreadful hill and approached the lifeless Jesus.

They worked in a rush as they wrapped his body. The sun was setting and the Jewish Passover was about to begin. There were rules about such things, and it was rules that mattered most to their religious sect. With Joseph's tomb so close by, he permitted Jesus' body to rest on the place reserved for his own. In a freshly hewn rock, where death had never been, they laid the forgiving flesh. The two Marys sat opposite the entrance and watched.

As you watch with them the ultimate incongruity that is the burial of Jesus Christ, there's more than meets the eye. They lift one arm, then the other. They fold them across his still chest, tuck in the spices, and mercifully cover his face, so taken over by death it is barely recognizable. While they do these things, know this: the Passover was the highest celebration in the life of a Jewish man, especially in the lives of privileged leaders such as these. When you look at Joseph and Nicodemus from now on, see two old Pharisees who just gave their Passover away. They wouldn't be taking part . . . not that year . . . not after the way they had handled the dead body of Jesus.

These two who loved their rules must have loved Jesus more.

Do you see it there against the backdrop of Golgotha? There, so close to the battered and breathless body of God, was the release of something new.

(Please read John 19:38-42.)

Some people have a problem with Christianity that can be stated like this: "I'm a positive person. My philosophy is to see the bright and lovely side of life. Christianity is always talking about sinning and repenting, always making rules and judgments, always imposing guilt and fear. 'People are bad and going to hell' and 'the world is evil' and 'we're all dying' . . . frankly, it turns me off. I don't need the negativity bringing me down."

This objection deserves a thoughtful answer. It's the apostle Paul himself, under divine inspiration, who counsels us that "whatever is noble, whatever is right . . . whatever is lovely . . . think about such things." By all means think about those things, "and the God of peace will be with you."[183] However, do you know what adjective actually appears first on his list?

"Whatever is true . . ."

You want to think positive thoughts? Good. But this is first: they must be true. Positive thinking cannot mean pretending—being unwilling to see painful realities. (By the way, we are all dying.) A personal philosophy of squeezing your eyes shut to the things that you do not want to see, if you can manage it, could seem to work for a while.

Spiritually speaking, it will kill you.

When ugly grasshoppers had eaten everything in sight, devastating ancient Israel, the people asked the prophet Joel what they should do. His answer? "Weep!" "Wail!" "Mourn!"[184]

His answer was not, "Look on the bright side." It was not, "Stay positive." In fact, no response was called for but that they open their eyes, see what they had become before God, and let the painful truth in.

Think of all the means God has used to open people up to truths they never wanted to see—truths about the world, about life, about themselves. He wrote pain into their child-bearing. He planted thorns in their soil. Waters ravaged the ugly world. Fire fell from the sky. He permitted the evil hiding within people to be expressed in openly evil acts. He let the ground open up at their feet. He sent prophets to shout at them and enemies to carry them away . . . all to show them their own desperate conditions. The news was worse than they could have imagined. They had a problem with sin, which meant they had a problem with God. For this reason they lived in a world for which no one is truly equipped, among horrible dangers and far, far from home.

The Israelites answered their prophet Joel, "Tell us pleasant things . . . and stop confronting us with the Holy One of Israel!"[185] Sound familiar?

So, to reach them, there was one thing God had never done before.

From now on, if the idea begins to appeal to you that there is nothing so much wrong with life, with the world, or with you and me that thinking differently can't solve, think about this: God lying there dead—brutalized, butchered, murdered by this world.

Whatever was really wrong with everything, measure its weight by the fact that this was the only solution: God, in the person of Christ his Son, lying there dead. I am convinced that the only solution to my life, which God can always see just as it is, no matter how nice I make it appear to you, was my Lord Christ lying there dead. Yet out of the most awful thing we could ever confront comes the most beautiful.

It's something like what the grief counselor means by the word *closure*. It can be important for family members to see the body of their loved one to help them accept the fact and achieve closure: "Okay then. So it's really over. So it's really done." In this way we come to the public death of the Son of God while hundreds stood staring. All four of the gospels call us to come close and watch. Sit there with the two Marys. Draw near to the funeral of the Lord, because here is closure . . . on the matter of all your sin, your guilt, your grievous and unending hell.

"So it's really over then. So it's really done."

Yes. For he was, for a time, really dead.

Christianity is never mere positive thinking alone. It's always thinking that turns positive in the end. It always starts with some profoundly disturbing truths. If you'll see them, if you can handle, so to speak, what God himself is showing you by his Word—and only then—they will give way to other truths, exhilarating truths that make you alive and set you free.[186] That's the way it works. Forgiveness makes me come alive precisely because I still see my sin. I celebrate the gifts of faith and love in the people I'm with, for the very reason that I've seen what we are like if left to ourselves. Heaven fills me with longing and hope to whatever degree I've seen this world as it really is. The truths of Christianity get up and dance to the degree I get it: I'm a sinner who is going to die.

But there stands Jesus.

Everything that it meant for the two Marys to see him alive that one particular Sunday morning came to them entirely because they had first seen him die. So, in Christ, there is an eternal optimism and a joy that doesn't depend on you closing your eyes to any painful thing. Whatever God wants you to see during this life, which he will gently but relentlessly show you, there will always be forgiveness on the other side. There will always be his Spirit holding you together. There will always be heaven standing open, waiting inevitably, more beautiful than your mind can conceive. When a personal philosophy of positive thinking leaves you cold because you're dying and you're scared, think with me of Jesus—so noble, so right, so lovely, and, best of all, so true. He lives! You need no other affirmation than this!

Here is all my resilience, and yours if you do not refuse to believe. It lies in knowing that whatever valleys the river of your life will run through, in the end it will empty out into heavenly glory.

You only think of Jesus, and you are positive.

Consider an analogy from C. S. Lewis. A hundred people went to live in the same building. However, 50 of them were told the place was a hotel, and 50 were told it was a prison. Ironically, those who held the positive view became the bitter ones: "What kind of hotel is this!? It's drafty and smelly and . . ." You get the idea.

On the other hand, the 50 who seemed to have the pessimistic view were pleasantly surprised. "Hmmmm. Spacious rooms. Fully furnished. The plumbing works. You know, for a prison . . . it's not bad!"

And so, it is precisely those who naively try to maintain a positive view—as if the world is designed to make them happy, as if people are basically good—who wind up in cynicism and tears. "What's the matter with this place? What's wrong with these people? It's not supposed to be like this!"

A hotel? The followers of Jesus have no such illusions about the world or about themselves. The biblical view is of that most awful ground from which grows beauty, gratitude, and joy. Given the life I should expect in a world moaning with sin and overwhelmed by death—given what I must be prepared for even now—I live among unexpected surprises, unbearably sweet.

My comfortable home and meaningful work—which of these did I deserve?

The love of family and friends—something only God could have given.

This faith, this hope, this inexpressible joy that stirs to life as I sit staring at Christ.

You know, for a prison, it's not bad!

"How can you believe he rose from the dead?"

Once seven demons had wrapped themselves around Mary Magdalene's soul. That was before Jesus. What had that torment been like, or that release? Think of it to understand how she felt about Jesus . . . and how she felt when a Roman soldier made sure he was good and dead. That, by the way, is one thing Romans carrying spears know how to do. The Christ was really dead.

That was Friday.

Now it's Sunday.

Mary left the house when it was still dark to go and anoint his corpse. But when she reached the burial place, there was nothing to do but stand there and cry. The body was missing. When it had seemed that things could get no worse, that there was nothing left to be taken from her, even his body was gone.

"Sir," she said to a man standing by, "if you have carried him away, tell me where you have put him, and I will get him." This pathetic, heroic plea—as if she were going to hoist his dead weight over her shoulders all by herself. That wouldn't be necessary.

He said, "Mary."

What he said next was, "Do not hold on to me," because that's what she was doing. She was holding Jesus, clutching him, not letting him go, not this time.

And isn't this the very instant we are always needing to get back to: What was the Christian faith in that instant, when Mary's arms wrapped around Jesus, alive just a few feet from his grave? It's a question designed to sweep away two thousand intervening years as if they were nothing at all.

What did it mean to be a Christian just then, at that single, incredible moment?

I imagine Mary's mind could only slowly open up to a thing so immense, or it could only open up slowly to her. It would take a little time for her soul to wrap itself around this . . . and everything that was given back to her . . . when he said, "Mary."

(Please read John 20:1-18.)

Maybe Jesus didn't really die. Maybe he passed out on the cross and later, inside the tomb, recovered and got away. Or perhaps his followers stole his body and spread the story that he was alive. Maybe he had a twin brother that made an appearance or two after Jesus died. Maybe some sort of mass hypnosis took hold, or some huge and extraordinarily clever conspiracy. Or could all this be just a legend that developed many years later? Yes, there are gaping holes in the logic of all these theories, and many competent historians have driven large automobiles through them. Still, aren't these explanations, weak as they are, more plausible than the story written by John?

Without implying that our faith is merely a judgment we make concerning historical evidence, I would still point out that these theories have none. In fact, they run contrary to all the evidence that we have. What evidence? We have the written eyewitness testimonies of those who were present, who gave the rest of their lives to the telling, and who called it joy to spill their blood rather than let go the simple words, "Jesus lives!" Consider that when they claimed to have seen Jesus physically raised from the dead, they were making the most difficult and dangerous case they could have imagined, if it were not true. Since the disciples had demonstrated their belief in ghosts on other occasions, a naïve leftover from their former spiritual confusion, the easiest and most natural fabrication would have been to say that they had been met by the spirit of Jesus. This isn't what they ran shouting at all. Their startling reports of a bodily resurrection, supported by the detailed descriptions of having touched Jesus and even of having seen him eat, meant making a claim that could have been easily demolished if it were not the simple truth. The powerful enemies of Jesus that wanted nothing more than to make this Christ go away—that would have loved to have "smothered Christianity in its cradle"[187]—only needed to come up with his body. They didn't.

Instead they took their best shot and tried to circulate a story that, even from our distant vantage point, is simply not credible. Terrified disciples, without motive (it's clear they never expected an actual resurrection but were persuaded in spite of their assumptions), converged on a position guarded by Romans? Luckily, the Roman guards (oblivious and unashamed of the capital offense) were napping?

This is the best they could do?

Elsewhere in this book, I have dealt with the issue of the overwhelming credibility of those apostles and what they wrote. It will suffice to say that any historian will tell you that there is no better category of historical verification than letters and similar documents written by contemporary witnesses of the events in question. This is the character of the entire New Testament. The evidence becomes overwhelming, from the historian's point of view, when it is recognized that those documents were widely disseminated and received as credible at a time when thousands were still living who could have discredited them. To borrow a phrase from Sherlock Holmes, this deafening silence has been called history's greatest example of "the dog that didn't bark."

Further, just try explaining away the monumental shift from the Jewish Sabbath to Sunday as the day of worship, which can be traced back to Jerusalem around the time of Christ's resurrection. Next, try explaining the stunning about-face in the life of an ingenious man named Paul (well known to history), apart from the explanation he himself gave—that he met the risen Lord on the road to Damascus. He had every conceivable motivation to expose Christ as a hoax and the intellectual brilliance to do so if he could have. He did not. And if all that were not enough, we have the existence of the Christian church itself. It is simply a fact. Before Easter the church consisted of little more than a few frightened followers locked in a room. It exploded into existence and wrapped its arms around the known world only after the death of its charismatic founder. The death-defying confession of untold thousands could not have been inspired by a broken casualty or by a half-dead man who somehow crawled away from a crucifixion. You say, "People die for silly causes all the time"? Not like this. These people were in a position, historically speaking, to know with a certainty whether it was all true or not.

It's not a hallucination, or a clever twin, you're thinking of as you choose to follow him through fire. You don't select "Christ is risen indeed!" for your last words based on a shaky lie or a fireside story. Clearly something extraordinary happened!

The Christian church is simply fact. And it is . . . because Christ is. The miraculous emergence of the church in the face of brutal Roman persecution, in the vivid words of C. F. D. Moule, "rips a great hole in history, a hole the size and shape of Resurrection."

Consider the uniqueness and the audacity of the claim of Christ himself before he died. When asked why he ought to be listened to, what proof he would offer, he clearly lined himself up with ancient prophetic Scriptures and repeatedly predicted his own resurrection from the grave. He was willing to say, in effect, "Believe in me when you see me alive after I've died." What movement in history has ever hinged on someone's ability to make good on such an all-or-nothing claim?

Many highly credentialed historians, including B. F. Westcott and Henry Morris, do not blush to call the resurrection of Christ the most certain fact in history, and this according to the established standards of historical verification.[188] It need not strain at all to pass every accepted test for determining the best explanation of a body of historical facts.[189] With all this evidence, is it really the Christian who believes whatever he wants to believe in spite of all evidence to the contrary? Far from it! The swoon theory, the notion that all five hundred who saw him alive at once shared a hallucination, and all the other attempts to get Jesus back into the ground—these are the complete and utter fabrications. It is these notions that have nothing whatever to do with even the tiniest shred of evidence. And I ask, Why? If someone is an honest searcher for the truth, if someone pretends to care about a reasonable weighing of evidence, why keep trying to evade that to which all the evidence points? When you think of it, all the truth of Easter really requires to be plausible is the condition that God exists.

"For nothing is impossible with God."[190]

I must confess, however, that I haven't yet explained my own faith. It is the truth itself, as the Scripture brings it to me and as the Spirit moves through the words, that is the real reason I believe.

You see, we are dying, you and I. There's not one single thing we can do about it. And we secretly understand that it's our own fault, that there is unspeakable shame in our dying, and that it comes to us because we are unacceptable to God. Our truer instincts, known as conscience and the natural knowledge of God, have become to us demons that are impossible to shake. And if we die and are nothing in the end, then our lives are robbed of all true meaning and all motivation and all reason for living. We are wasted and undone by sin. We have nothing.

During one particularly painful time in my life, night after night I would deliberately fall asleep in the moment from John chapter 20 that I described at the beginning of this chapter. It held me together—how two angels were sitting where Jesus' head and feet were supposed to be. And Mary cried, for she had lost the world. But then these words turned her around: "Why are you crying?" And they also turn me. This is the gift: that the Spirit can take us there, that two thousand intervening years do become nothing at all, and that by faith I am face-to-face with God.

I have believed in him alive all my life, yet I still explore the landscape here on the other side of Easter. My mind slowly opens. This new light slowly dawns.

If Jesus lives, what then?

Then everything he ever said is true. Then everything he ever claimed to be he is. Then everything he ever promised will come. Then my Uncle Norb, my Aunt Marie, my cousin Ruth, who died in a crash—all my dear ones in Jesus—are still mine. Then there is every reason to wait, to hope, to endure. Then there is love like this at the center of all things, and forever in this love I will rest.

And so it goes, on and on and on.

I am still opening up to it, and it to me . . . everything that was given back to me . . . when he said, "Mary."

"How do I know I'm a Christian?"

You didn't realize how much you had come to count on him . . . until they took him away. They brutalized him, led him out of the city, and nailed him up there. It was beyond cruel what they did to him. It was grotesque. And that's how he died. Believe me, you hadn't counted on that.

That was two days ago. You pull a friend aside. "Let's get out of here." You just want to think. You want to sort it all out. "Let's go home."

The unthinkable fills your conversation as you two walk the seven miles down from the rocky barrenness of Jerusalem through that lovely valley toward Emmaus. You think you're alone, but a Stranger calls, "What are you discussing together as you walk along?"

What is everyone talking about? Doesn't he know the things that happened in Jerusalem?

"What things?"

The truth is, this Stranger knows what he thinks happened in Jerusalem in the last couple of days. He wants to know what you think. You talk to Jesus about Jesus, saying, "We had hoped that he was the one who was going to redeem Israel."

What you really mean is, "That was before."

And for that he calls you a fool—a gentle rebuke that names

the source of all your despair. You are painfully slow to believe even the things that come from God.

Then he begins quoting his Bible until the entire Old Testament Scripture falls open as a book about Jesus. "Didn't the Christ have to suffer these things and then enter his glory?" How had you not seen that before? And this new warmth in your chest doesn't come from recognizing the Stranger walking beside you. You don't. But you are recognizing Jesus in the Word. And this is not, as you might think, an inferior way of finding him compared to seeing him face-to-face. It is now, discovering him in the Word, that you finally understand him. You finally know him.

"So . . . he had to die . . . for fools and unbelievers, he had to die."

Emmaus comes up on you all too quickly, but not before your slow-warming heart has caught on fire. You persuade him to stay the night. Once in your home, your guest becomes the host. Reaching for the bread, he gives thanks, breaks it, and holds it out to you. And at the moment that gives him the most pleasure to do it, he pulls away the veil, and you suddenly see him. Jesus!

He disappears, and in a moment you're out the door on the seven-mile trek back to Jerusalem, back to your friends. You run the whole way, crying, "I'm a Christian."

No, that's not what you're saying. You aren't thinking of yourself at all. What is filling your mind is, "He is risen. It's all true. He was seen by us when he broke the bread!" You don't run back to Jerusalem crying, "I am a Christian now."

You just are.

(Please read Luke 24:13-35.)

How do I know I am a Christian? How can I recognize that it has definitely happened to me? How do I recognize this genuine, living, saving faith when it lives in me?

The thing to notice about that first question is the way it turns you inward. The question gets you examining yourself and your own experience. Personally speaking, the longer I spend at this, asking questions about myself—just how strong is my belief, how renewed is my life—the less sure I become. In every aspect of my life, I'll find things that sure look like unbelief, things that sure smell like death, and the evidence against me is always the easier to spot. I can say, "I really, really believe," and I do, but someone who knows me at my worst only has to say, "Do you?" Looking at me makes even me wonder.

So how do I know I have the faith of a true Christian?

Let's not worry about that just now. Let's set that question aside. For the moment let's not talk about faith at all. Let me ask something else of you, assuming you've stayed with my little book this far. What has God done about the sin of the world? Has God found a way to make you acceptable in his sight? Has God left anything out when it comes to being your Savior? Stop asking yourself, "What is in my heart?" Ask, "What is in his?"

I want you to notice what I'm doing. I am setting aside the questions that turn you inward. It's important to understand that your assurance never comes from the look inside. I mean never. We are, after all, just sinners.

I deliberately ask the questions that turn your thoughts away from yourself toward the God who has redeemed his people. What has God done about your sin? The answer is Jesus, dying in shame not his own. How has God made you acceptable? The answer is Jesus, alive from the dead. Has he not said it right there in his Word, "I have loved you with an everlasting love"?[191] The healing answer is yes.

We must take great care to ask the right questions, those answered on the cross, where he died in that horrible way just for us. We deliberately ask the questions that were put to rest when he appeared alive. We ask the questions that are settled as matters of unchangeable historical fact. We ask the questions that are answered factually and objectively on the black-and-white pages of Holy Scripture. What about all my sin?

"The LORD has taken away your sin."[192]

Think about Jesus and the way he died. The Word, from beginning to end, cries out, "Take this. This is for you." What is now in God's heart toward you? That is the question for God and only God to answer. And that he does with the Word, by the water, and in the bread and wine.

"I am for you! I am with you! I am Christ your Savior, alive for ever and ever!"

If there is any joy in you now, it is the joy of a Christian. If any peace, any "thank you, Jesus" is stirred up in you, the world knows nothing about it, only you who happen to believe him know anything about it. If you're standing where I stand now, you aren't thinking, "I'm a Christian now." You just are.

You look to yourself and all you see is sin and death. You look for faith and it seems to elude you, because faith was not made to look at itself. It does not mean looking within. Faith means looking away from yourself. There in Jesus you see everything you need. I continually find that when my faith is burning brightest, I am not thinking of faith at all.

Everything is Christ.

How do I know I am a Christian? Change the question: How do I know God loves even me? Faith—genuine, true, alive—answers, "Jesus." Are you left to yourself to manufacture this conviction in yourself? No, it is the gift of God, the work of his Holy Spirit by means of his powerful Word.

Is it possible that you, in repentance over sin, could desire this gift and that he could refuse to give it to you? The desire itself is the first stirring of spiritual life, so don't be afraid.

After all, what made Jesus walk those miles to Emmaus on the day of his resurrection from the dead? He had come a lot further than that for those two men. Do you wish you could believe in him? He wants you more. You would not desire him if he weren't first drawing you in with cords of everlasting love.

If I could be with you now, all I would do is turn my Bible toward you—John chapter 1 or Ephesians chapter 2 or 2 Corinthians chapter 5. I would say, "Here . . . just read from here to here. . . . I'll wait." It is, after all, the Father's greatest pleasure to reveal Christ his Son.

I tried to explain forgiveness to Lisa in every way I could think of. I explained it using my best analogies. I explained forgiveness with my favorite sermon illustrations. I explained it in Hebrew, Greek, and English. The thing is, she always knew what I meant. She just found it hard to believe. There was so much shame.

I'm not saying my explanations weren't good and biblical ones. Simply put, faith remains God's gift to give. Jesus prepares the moment of deepest, holiest pleasure when God himself pulls back the veil.

I thought about Jesus when he stole into the room, alive from the dead. He breathed on his disciples—*"hhh-hhhhhhhh"*—and said, "If you forgive anyone his sins, they are forgiven."[193] So I stopped talking about forgiveness. I just looked into her eyes . . . and forgave her.

"Lisa, in Jesus' name, I forgive you."

She didn't smile back and announce, "Oh, I get it. I'm a Christian now."

She started to cry.

It was the last time they would see Jesus in this world, save in their dreams—one lasting impression to sustain them through God knows what, for the rest of their lives.

He stood there, death all behind him, love in his eyes, scarred hands lifted up . . . blessing them. The image is the gospel itself—what we could never have earned or deserved—God standing there with benediction. We are never cursed, never condemned, never given to endure the living God's face turned angry and away. We are blessed.

The last thing Jesus said was, "You will be my witnesses . . ." and with that he was taken from their sight, lifted from the Mount of Olives, and held for a moment in the expanse until a cloud hid him from sight. He left his disciples standing on this hill with their heads thrown back toward heaven, squinting at the sky, faces filling up with the expanse of blue and white, until angels interrupted, "Why do you stand here looking into the sky?"

The angels didn't merely say, "Jesus will come back." There's one other little word not to be missed. It's a priceless word when you call to mind the gospel stories. The angels said, "This *same* Jesus . . . will come back in the same way."

Won't you look up with me on some partly cloudy day and let the words drift softly through your mind?

"Come to me, all you who are weary."

"Neither do I condemn you."

"Little girl, get up!"

"This same Jesus . . ."

(Please read Luke 24:50-53; Acts 1:1-11.)

When I'm jogging, when my legs ache and my chest is on fire, I'll sometimes throw my head back, all the way back. It's a fairly interesting effect. Suddenly houses and cars, fences and mailboxes, and especially the long stretch of road I have yet to run, all just disappear. All I see is sky. Only the blue fills my vision. It's a metaphor for an approach to life that the Bible consistently calls us toward. Simply put, "Look up!"

"Set your hearts on things above, where Christ is seated at the right hand of God."[194]

We are in a race, and we will be tired and hurting right up to the moment the tape is broken. So often this world and the mess we're in here, where we are always sinning and always dying, are all we see. What if we could learn to throw our heads back, spiritually speaking, to let heaven fill our vision, to have thoughts of glory be the deepest-worn paths in our minds, to long for the waiting joy, to focus outright on eternity? What if we fully embraced the reality of heaven and reveled in the inevitability of you and me being there through Christ? What if we let this become our resilience and our unforced smiles? Could we live for heaven to such a degree that we could rise above the disappointment here?

Go even further. Could we live as if we are nobodies on earth—as if we're not even here at all but are somehow already there? We have already been "seated . . . with [Christ] in the heavenly realms,"[195] wrote the apostle Paul. Is this the key to an effective life even now? Or does our upward gaze only make us rather useless here and look like yokels besides?

This is one of the world's complaints about Christians— our heads are in the clouds. We only want to go to heaven, so we're not up to doing the practical things that need to be done today. One interesting thing about this objection is that it has no basis in reality. Think about our own country's history. Just who founded the hospitals? Who established the great universities? Whose ideas were the great charitable institutions that have endured? Where have the arts always flourished? Where did the moral authority come from to end slavery? Where did the civil rights movement get its strength and compass from? Who is almost exclusively trying to save the lives of unborn babies? Who blesses marriage? Who heals the sick, cares for the poor, or repents that he or she is not doing so enough?

Need I go on? The answer is people of the Christian faith.

Recognize a paradox? The heavenly minded, those with their heads in the clouds, have so often been the ones making significant differences for good in this world. This seeming contradiction goes all the way back to the apostles, who said, "Set your hearts on things above, where Christ is,"[196] and with faces aimed at heaven, they changed the world. We could stand to be *more* heavenly minded.

It's being earthly minded that does not work. People are like unlit lightbulbs looking for some place to plug themselves in, searching for that something that will light them up. They can plug in to their friends or their spouses or their children to make them happy. But ultimately this ugly demand will color their most important relationships: "Someone come through for me! Make me happy! Meet my need!" They can plug in to success or pleasure, money or possessions to try to somehow feel alive, to feel that they're special. But death creeps close to all people the same way, to tell them they're not special after all and to peel back each clutching finger. They reach in vain for anything available to make the aches go away—drugs, alcohol, promiscuous sex—and take destruction into their own hands.

It is God in heaven who made us, but I do not naturally plug in to the Father to find my life either. By nature I didn't want to and wouldn't have known how if I had wanted to. Of this I am ashamed. Then I see Jesus alive in these Scriptures, forgiveness in his eyes, pierced palms spread over me in blessing. These are the feet once nailed to the wood. These are the hands that have written one very good word behind all my pain: *temporary.* And behind everything my thirsty heart knows how to thirst for, and so much more it hasn't even dreamed of, he has written his exhilarating "forever."

We're just going to have to trust him.

As Christian psychologist Larry Crabb says, life itself is not about "a plan to follow," that is, a plan to fix whatever is wrong here. It's about "a person to trust."[197]

That person is Jesus.

"Remain in me,"[198] he whispers.

So let me live with one foot in the air. Let me hear my Father's footsteps in the hall, closer now than when I first believed. I do not ignore or deny the sorrow of this world. It is not necessarily a weakness in my faith when I am sad. Another beautiful insight from Crabb is simplicity itself: I am "legitimately longing for heaven."[199] I am homesick for a place I've never been and aching for a face I've never seen, in which is hidden everything I've been designed to enjoy. The joy lies in knowing that I certainly will stand in that place and see that face at last.

You may question the doctrine, but not the effect it has on me. The reality of that fixed moment is already reaching into the life I live in this world, lighting the joy that hides within every soon-ending sorrow. Not long and I'll be home. Entirely on the coattails of Christ, I will arrive safely into glory. I rest myself in this knowledge, and I wait.

Wait with me.

Don't judge God based on your life experiences in the split second of time you lived under his enemy's flag. Withhold the judgment your unbelieving heart wants to make based on the things you see in this world—his master-piece ruined by sin and death. These were never the plan. The beauty that remains is a whiff of another country, a heavenly one, where everything is just as it should be for-ever. Some things just won't be right until we're home. So wait and see. Let the story end. Simply believe in him . . . and look up.

Knowing that Christ is the way to a place called heaven is precisely what is required if I am to do any real, lasting good on earth. I'll fix my eyes on Jesus. I'll throw my head back. I'll rise above all of this. I'll fill up my eyes with glory.

And at the lunch table where I work, at the funeral of a friend, at the bedsides of my little girls . . . I will be his witness.

Men blinded by rage surrounded him, their hearts full of violence, their hands groping for him and for the near-est stone. That's when Stephen looked up.

"I see heaven open and the Son of Man standing at the right hand of God."[200]

We are accustomed to hearing about Jesus *sitting* at the right hand of God. But Stephen was shouting his witness above the angry cries. The first martyr was surrendering his body to the first persecutors.

And Jesus stood up.

What we see in Stephen is what he learned from Jesus. He learned to live in an unearthly way. "Lord, do not hold this sin against them." And he learned to die well, abandoning himself to Christ with something like a bedtime prayer, "Lord Jesus, receive my spirit."

He fixed his mind on things above . . . where Christ is.

The gospel according to Luke records the miraculous birth of Christ in Bethlehem. In his sequel, the book of Acts, Luke treats the miraculous birth of Christ's church in places like Corinth, Philippi, and Ephesus. Here we witness Jesus "born into the world" in a new way, following his ascension into heaven. His Spirit delivers him into the lives of those who believe in him; he is revealed all over again in the new Christlike love the believers have for one another.

Three thousand people in the city that rejected the Son of God find out that he is real after all, that he is alive—"O God, what now?"—and that he forgives them. Into this peace they, with their little ones, are baptized.

In a community characterized by prayer and praise, togetherness and generosity form around the Word of Christ. Those who still stand outside can only admire what they see within. The number of the saved-by-grace daily swells.

A man named Paul, dedicated body and soul to the destruction of this church, is confronted by the living Christ on the road to Damascus. He is struck by a blinding light and knocked to the ground by the awfulness of that for which he had been most proud—he had killed the followers of Jesus. Yet there is grace even for him and water to wash even such ugliness away.

So began his journey to tell the whole world about the redemption he found in the blood of Jesus. I wonder. What was it like to be let down from the walls of Damascus in a basket at night? Did Paul smile to himself as he was suspended for a moment, swaying in the dark, making his escape from his former way of life?

I wonder and I ask, Who are all these people?

Not angels from heaven. Not people appearing perfect in every way. They are the people of faith—repentant, forgiven, grateful, growing—and they happen to love one another.

Now the thing about history, as they say, is that it repeats. When a thing has happened once, the world is never safe from it happening again.

It is through the saved ones, such as they are, that the Savior is known. Then he comes.

(Please read Acts 2:1-47; 9:1-31.)

The atheist challenges, "Christians have to look a lot more saved before I'll believe in their Savior." People echo that sentiment for any number of reasons. They have bristled at the blatant hypocrisy of the televangelists. They have had hurtful experiences in the church and still lick the wounds. They have met obnoxious Christians and didn't feel the love in these people's relentless pursuits to convert them.

This is what it means to be saved?

I admit that church advertising gets downright silly. "Come meet the most loving people ever" is foolish, unchristian boasting. If we belong to Christ, we are capable of genuine sorrow over our dismal failures to reflect him well. I bring no excuse. It's staggering to realize that he allows the world to cast its verdict on him by what they see in the likes of us. Please don't walk away on account of me. I say, with Dostoyevsky, "Attack me, not the path I so poorly follow."

In fact, may I say again that the question on which your soul depends is the one about Jesus? Who do you say *he* is? Don't let a few people you don't like keep you from the One who loves you as no one else can. Watchman Nee observed that God has not given many separate gifts to the world—love, joy, peace, hope—but one gift, Jesus. In him is everything else contained. Everything. The superiority you feel over Christians—go ahead and admit it—is a dismal reason to miss out on Christ.

Please consider all the reasons why judging the merits of Christianity by the outward appearance of Christians is suspect. Understand that the Christian faith is by definition an inner light and life. How is it supposed to look? The sorrow that comes from God, the faith that saves and connects us to Christ as so many parts of his body, and the impulses to love that come from this Head move beneath the waterline. Sometimes they barely make themselves known beneath the same old damnable flesh that is common to all people, Christian or not. Our Christian life is "hidden with Christ in God."[201]

Notice how one selfish man justifies his self-centeredness as a legitimate way to live, while another privately grieves over it and clings to Christ inwardly . . . and you would never know. Compare the first man and his same old, same old struggle to be good enough with the second man who endeavors to say thank you to God with his forgiven life. All you may see on the outside is that both strive. The one does good things to get God to love him; the other does them because God already does.

At first glance they are indistinguishable.

Although these two don't appear to be standing on opposite sides of a great divide, they are. The one who believes in Jesus has already "crossed over from death to life."[202] And because of the slow, hidden work of the Holy Spirit, I say that you can find Christ being revealed in that second life—the repentant one, the grateful one.

Consider the Christian man who struggles with a particularly abrasive temperament. Not one thing in all of Christian theology is threatened by the fact that he really does believe and that he really does struggle. However, under the category of things you cannot see, you must include what sort of man he would have been without Christ and what sort of man he will yet become as God's work in progress. Most of all, if it is appearances that impress you, take into account the difference that judgment day will make when the "sons of God [will] be revealed."[203] When the hidden Christ appears, then we Christians will appear with him in glory.

I expect we'll look sufficiently saved then.

In the meantime, Christianity is best understood as a thing centering on Christ. If you ask to see my salvation, it's him I will point to, not myself. This pointing to Jesus, out of the sorrow and gratitude that is my daily existence, well, it is as "saved" as I know how to look. Though I don't seem like much to you or, for that matter, to me, the miracle and the thing that matters most is how I look to God. "I am a dunghill covered with snow."[204] I am covered in Jesus' righteousness, just by faith in his blood. This Christian church, the body of all who trust in him, is Christ's waiting, gleaming bride.

"Christ loved the church and gave himself up for her . . . to present her to himself as a radiant church, without stain or wrinkle or any other blemish, but holy and blameless."[205]

Mystery of mysteries, grace upon grace, we are beautiful to him.

And through the likes of hopelessly flawed Christians like me, people are being safely gathered into God and into

God's church through the message about salvation in Jesus Christ. This act of gathering is what God has been up to and what history has been about right from the start. In the end we are glorious.

Even now, for all our weakness and seeming ordinariness, we know him. The flat-out best thing about us—our ability to bring profound blessing to the whole world—lies in the fact that we carry inside the message of that world brought back to God in Christ. We are dispensable clay jars concealing gleaming treasure. We are the lights in a darkening world, such as we are. The Word of Christ makes us so.

You are wondering if there is any such thing as love in the world. In these cynical times, you are looking for the real thing, for living and breathing, walking and talking love. That's Jesus. The truth is that there have been people, countless people, who knew him well and gladly gave all they had in service to the world. They let the human need all around them break their hearts. They spent themselves in their compassionate responses. Then they laid down their lives rather than let go of their holds on Christ.

For "the world was not worthy of them,"[206] chimed in the Lord of glory himself.

Lord of the church, Father of lights, Spirit of God, let that also be me.

On an island called Patmos, when only John was left alive of the Twelve, Jesus came with eyes like fire and face like sunlight. "I was dead, and behold I am alive for ever and ever."[207] He appeared as one standing among the lampstands, that is, the churches. He brought a message we call the book of Revelation, through the disciple he loved.

You are critical of Christ's church? Guess what? So is Christ. "You have forsaken your first love,"[208] he told the Christians in Ephesus. "Lukewarm,"[209] he called the congregation in a place called Laodicea. After all, he is the one that has the right to criticize the church. You see, he happens to love her. He saved her.

She is his.

You look for genuine faith and something that can truly be called love to be found somewhere in her? He does too. And by his own grace and power, he finds them. "You have not denied my name," he tells her. "Be faithful, even to the point of death, and I will give you the crown of life."[210]

How are we going to look then?

CONCLUSION

"Why stories?"

Breathe deep the spellbinding story from Jesus.

A son put as much ground as he could between himself and his father. He made all-grown-up choices. He did things he never thought he would do. There, so far away, having ruined everything that could be ruined, "he came to his senses."

Somewhere in his heart he sighed, "Daddy," and began the long walk home.

Meanwhile, the father watched for him, scanning the horizon day after day. The father saw the son from a distance, and don't you dare skim too quickly over this sparkling detail:

The father ran!

Now the young man had rehearsed for this moment. "I know it can never be the same. I should be your slave. Only let me . . ."

"My son!"

The forgiveness of sins—this is the teaching of our church and the pulse of our creed. It is good sound doctrine, the kind that keeps us alive to God. And this story? This is what it's like.

Forgiveness is the father rocking his son in the warmth of his embrace. "My son, my son, my son . . . I thought I'd lost you . . . oh my son." Forgiveness is the robe on a lost son's back, the ring on his finger, the sandals on his feet. It's the joyful sound of a party given for anyone at all, just for coming home. That's the look and scent and feel of forgiveness.

It's what I wanted to tell you but wasn't sure how. That is, until Jesus caught forgiveness like a living thing at play in the net of this brilliant story.

Take that long, slow look at the face of God as Jesus brings him close. No darkness appears on the Father's face, no brooding disapproval, not so much as a word about what the son had done. We mention our sins to God so that he never, never, never has to mention them to us.

May I let you in on the best-kept secret in the world? This is the Christian faith. Remain outside if you choose—"It's too easy! It's too free!" There's a joyful sound bursting from within, the delight of the Father at the party we call grace.

"We had to celebrate and be glad, for this son of mine was lost, but now is found. He was dead, but look. He is alive."

And the always-opened door is not merely the captivating story Jesus told.

It's the Storyteller himself.

(Please read Luke 15:11-32.)

Why tell stories? While you're pondering that, let this gleaming detail from the mine of Old Testament prophecy catch your eye—the Messiah himself would be a marvelous teller of stories.

Jesus did not say anything to the crowd without using a parable. "So was fulfilled what was spoken through the prophet: 'I will open my mouth in parables, I will utter things hidden since the creation of the world.' "[211]

I believe C. S. Lewis was on to something when it comes to the power of stories. He pointed out that every good narrative is made up of a series of events that make up the plot. But those successive moments—this happened, then that, then this—actually create a net in which the author is really trying to catch something else. In story, something is discovered that is not successive, such as what truth really is, or beauty, or friendship. So also the parables Jesus told were the net in which he captured for us such things as forgiveness, wisdom, faith . . . and love.

A father running toward the distant figure of his disgraced son.

A ring.

A robe.

A celebration.

Brought so close—made so clear amid the mesh—is a look at God's face. Jesus' parables let us wrap our thoughts around the deeper things—what the kingdom of God is like. We see it. We get it. We are let in.

The Scriptures say, "This is love: not that we loved God . . ."[212] Oh, we can keep up the hollow appearance of love. We can avoid the knowledge of the evil of which we are capable. We can let "psychological need seeking satisfaction"[213] pass for the real thing and keep on using the word *love* as a pious abstraction.

But we are not love's definition.

There is such a thing as love, but that ancient story doesn't go on to give a theological definition of *love*, per se. It conjures up the other story. "This is how we know what love is: Jesus Christ laid down his life for us."[214] Caught in that story—in the gambling for his clothes and in the thirst, in the sacrifice of a willing Substitute and in the spear that made sure he was good and dead—is "how we know what love is." In that true story, in those events that loom at the center of history, on a dark hill outside Jerusalem, is captured that very affection and grace that is the essence of God.

And so are captured all who believe. We are brought back alive in the net that is the real-life narrative about Jesus. The title? "You can always go home."

"My child, my child, my child . . . I thought I'd lost you . . . oh my child."

Yet I called it the best-kept secret in the world.

Friends, pause with me and survey this new territory, that is, the culture in which we now live. A college student reads the Sermon on the Mount and calls it "The most ridiculous thing I've ever heard." Do you know what that is? It's an honest first-century-like response to the shocking Christ from a young woman who is meeting him for the first time. Another woman walks into a jewelry store to buy a cross, and the clerk asks, "Do you want one with the little man on it?" She has no idea! For Jesus' sake, get over your being appalled at unbelievers just being unbelievers and see the opportunities.

We must expose them to what is unique about Christianity, namely, Christ. In today's culture the accounts of Jesus' life and ministry are fresh, untold stories. In my experience talking to people about Jesus, there still remains something both alarming and compelling about the Lord. Some hate him, some love him, but few can merely yawn and walk away.

It is for this reason that I've tried to model a very simple spirit in this book as I've dealt with objections to our Christian faith. I hope you have seen that it can be such a short and easy walk from any marginally religious conversation to a heart-pounding talk about Jesus. You tell the story you've been dying to tell. The Word is already hidden in your heart. The message of sin and grace is built right in.

"We are getting what our sins deserve. . . . Jesus, remember me," shouts the dying thief, when every breath was costly.

"You will be with me in paradise," answered God, when all was nearly done.

Yet I do need to be clear on one point. It is not as though storytelling could ever replace the need for the clearest possible articulation of Christian teaching. I'll admit that more and more people seem unprepared to deal seriously with doctrines as such and that this makes our job harder. To weigh the evidence of Scripture in order to accept or reject one truth claim or another—this just isn't how they think. Okay, so our job is harder.

People still need Christian doctrine, and they always will.

You see, in my experience, people often do not see with eyes fully opened to the meaning of the gospel until it is presented in a very explicit, formal presentation, such as "The Great Exchange" developed by seminary president David Valleskey. I am not ready to dispense with the pivotal role of clear witnessing that is done by means of clearly articulated teaching. To be somewhere nearby, to be in the same room, when objective justification has first become clear to someone against the backdrop of total depravity—this is the awesome moment of saving clarity that I am always working toward. This is still, in my view, the very best of the many conversations about Christ I need to have with people who do not know him.

But what will I say the next time we speak? And the time after that? Or how can I open the door with people in the first place? How can I speak openly and freely about Jesus no matter what jagged question mark hangs above the conversation? The beauty of casting the net of Bible stories is the way these stories supply the fodder for the numerous spiritual conversations you might need to have with a questioning soul before the truth breaks in. I've even found, every now and then, that I do not have to ask someone, "Do you mind if I share Christian teaching with you?" Sometimes a person has actually asked me for the finer points of our doctrine, having first seen a prostitute forgiven, a prodigal son welcomed home . . . or a good man whisper to a dead child, "Little girl, get up!"

There is a "rest of the story" when it comes to Kayla, whom I mentioned in the introduction to this book. There I told about the first time I met this woman at an appointment to have my hair cut. The next time I sat in her chair, she brought it up herself. She said, "Do you remember that story you told me about that little dead girl that Jesus brought to life?"

"Yes."

"Well, I told my husband!"

"What did he say?"

"Nothing. He just hugged me. And now he goes out of his way just to drive by your church. We've been talking about coming."

And there's more. The time after that we talked in the clearest terms about the death and resurrection of Jesus Christ and precisely what it means. It began with her asking me. When I was through with a very simple and clear presentation of the gospel, our eyes met in the mirror in front of us.

She said smiling, "So there are no hoops to jump through!"

"Yes, Kayla, that's it exactly. There are no hoops," I replied. For she spoke as one who gets it, who knows him, who has been caught in the net of the greatest story ever told. She saw him for the first time.

And in a way, so did I. I was let back in to the childhood of my faith. This is what makes my "joy complete,"[215] in a way no amount of internal struggle ever can. I had never been able to think myself back into the delight. Sitting and wrestling with my thoughts in my own private world of self-ish concerns—they had never brought me back.

Sitting in that chair, hearing that from her, it was all so simple again. It was all so clear. I embraced with both arms the story of Christ as I told it to someone else. I learned what the saying means: "I pray that you may be active in sharing your faith, so that you will have a full understanding of every good thing we have in Christ."[216]

Do you remember Jesus telling Peter to go back out in the heat of the day to the same lake where he had toiled and fished all night long and caught nothing?

He did, and this time the fish attacked the nets. And the fisherman, with his eyes slowly opening to Christ, fell, hiding his face and crying, "Go away from me, Lord; I am a sinful man."

Naturally, Jesus stood there for a moment, then helped him up.

He wasn't going anywhere.

He is with you too. He's the reason you row your little boat right back out onto the same old lake . . . to the same old spot where you've never caught a thing . . . when the time for fishing seems long past. A winsome smile, big as the sun, tells you who you are.

"Don't be afraid; from now on you will catch men."[217]

For Jesus' sake, in Jesus' name, lower the nets one more time.

ENDNOTES

[1] John 20:31

[2] Richard Trent, *Notes on the Parables of Our Lord* (Westwood, NJ: Fleming H. Revell Company, 1953), p. 26.

[3] Isaiah 49:15,16

[4] John 7:46

[5] Matthew 27:54

[6] Matthew 24:35

[7] Lee Strobel, *The Case for Faith* (Grand Rapids: Zondervan Publishing House, 2000), pp. 17,18.

[8] Revelation 22:20

[9] William Shakespeare, *Hamlet,* Act 1, Scene 5, lines 175-176.

[10] 1 Peter 1:21

[11] Gilbert K. Chesterton, *Orthodoxy* (Wheaton, IL: Harold Shaw Publishers, 1994), p. 65. My indebtedness to G. K. Chesterton goes beyond the various places he is quoted in this book.

[12] Genesis 1:1

[13] Josh McDowell, *The New Evidence That Demands a Verdict* (Nashville: Thomas Nelson Publishers, 1999), p. li.

[14] Josh McDowell, *The New Evidence That Demands a Verdict,* p. lii.

[15] Hugh Ross, *Design Evidences for Life Support: Probability Estimate for a Life Support Planet,* Pasadena: Reasons to Believe, 2000.

[16] Psalm 139:14

[17] Psalm 19:1

[18] Job 19:25

[19] Psalm 139:7,8

[20] Genesis 1:1

[21] Hebrews 1:3

[22] John 5:19

[23] Luke 1:35

[24] John 11:47,48

25Robert Knille, *As I Was Saying: A Chesterton Reader* (Grand Rapids: William B. Eerdmans Publishing Company, 1985), p. 267. This anthology lists "All is Grist" as the primary source.

26Gilbert K. Chesterton, *Orthodoxy,* p. 60.

27Psalm 139:14

28Psalm 139:13,15

29Lewis Thomas, *The Medusa and the Snail* (New York: Viking Press, 1979), pp. 155-157.

30Luke 3:1,2

31Paul L. Maier, *In the Fullness of Time* (San Francisco: A Division of HarperCollins Publishers, 1991), p. xvi.

32Luke 1:3,4

33Matthew 11:3

34John 20:18

35John 1:18

362 Peter 1:16

371 John 1:1

38Luke 2:2,7

39Adapted from Mark A. Paustian, "The iconoclast" (*Northwestern Lutheran,* December 1998), p. 18. Permission granted.

40Hebrews 1:3

412 Peter 3:8

42Isaiah 55:9

43John 18:4

44Matthew 28:20

45Job 42:3

46James 1:17

47Quoted in Philip Yancey, *Disappointment with God* (New York: HarperCollins Publishers, 1988), p. 311. I am indebted to Philip Yancey for this and other thoughts in this book.

48For some of the thoughts in this chapter, I am indebted to Ravi Zecharias, *Can Man Live without God,* Dallas: Word Publishing, 1994.

49Ireneaus, *Against Heresies,* Book IV, chapter 20, par. 7.

50Acts 17:30

51Isaiah 43:1

52John 20:29

53Psalm 73:25

[54]Isaiah 57:19

[55]John 17:4

[56]Luke 23:46

[57]Matthew 27:54

[58]John 17:10

[59]Quoted in Ravi Zecharias, *Can Man Live without God*, p. 39.

[60]Romans 2:15

[61]Quoted in Ravi Zecharias, *Can Man Live without God*, p. 40.

[62]Philip Yancey, *Disappointment with God*, p. 310.

[63]Luke 2:11

[64]Deuteronomy 6:4

[65]Colossians 2:9

[66]Acts 5:3,4

[67]1 John 4:8,16

[68]Based on Isaiah 6:1-4

[69]Matthew 27:46

[70]2 Corinthians 5:21

[71]Matthew 3:17

[72]Based on John chapter 17

[73]Matthew 9:2

[74]Ephesians 2:8

[75]John 19:30

[76]Romans 3:20

[77]Acts 13:39

[78]2 Corinthians 5:20

[79]1 Corinthians 13:3

[80]Genesis 2:23

[81]Robert Knille, *As I Was Saying: A Chesterton Reader*, p. 267. This anthology lists "The Defendant" as the primary source.

[82]Isaiah 62:5

[83]Taken from John 14:2,3

[84]Frederick Buechner, *Whistling in the Dark: An ABC Theologized* (San Francisco: HarperCollins Publishers, 1993), p. 22.

[85]Thought taken from 1 Peter 1:5

[86]Ephesians 3:18

[87]Based on Mark 4:35-41

[88]Acts 16:31

[89] Romans 12:19

[90] Luke 23:34

[91] John 6:63

[92] Matthew 26:14,25

[93] Genesis 3:10

[94] *Devotional Classics,* edited by Richard J. Foster and James Bryan Smith (San Francisco: Harper, 1993), p. 296.

[95] Matthew 18:20

[96] Based on Matthew 26:20-22

[97] Gilbert K. Chesterton, *Orthodoxy,* p. 103.

[98] 2 Corinthians 5:21

[99] John 19:30

[100] Hebrews 10:31

[101] Jeremiah 23:31

[102] Romans 6:23

[103] Psalm 119:105

[104] C. S. Lewis, *God in the Dock* (Grand Rapids: William B. Eerdmans Publishing Co., 1970), p. 204. I am indebted to C. S. Lewis for this and other thoughts in this book.

[105] Romans 3:2

[106] 2 Peter 1:19

[107] Matthew 17:5

[108] Philip Yancey, *Disappointment with God,* p. 43.

[109] Galatians 5:6

[110] John 12:32

[111] Matthew 11:28

[112] Romans 5:6

[113] Psalm 73:25

[114] 2 Corinthians 12:10

[115] Isaiah 40:29,31

[116] Genesis 32:26

[117] Luke 18:1

[118] Adapted from Mark A. Paustian, "Drinking our cup" (*Forward in Christ,* March 2000), pp. 18,19. Permission granted.

[119] Matthew 27:46

[120] Isaiah 9:6 (KJV)

[121] Adapted from John 14:2

[122]2 Corinthians 4:17

[123]John 18:11

[124]Adapted from Mark Paustian, "Drinking our cup," pp. 18,19. Permission granted. (I'm indebted to author Henri Nouen for these thoughts on "drinking our cup.")

[125]Translations in this section are based on the original Greek.

[126]Matthew 7:23

[127]Ravi Zecharias, *Can Man Live without God*, p. 25.

[128]Zecharias, p. 23.

[129]1 John 4:16

[130]Matthew 5:44

[131]Luke 6:27

[132]Romans 12:14

[133]John 3:17

[134]Robert Knille, *As I Was Saying: A Chesterton Reader*, p. 268. This anthology lists *The Everlasting Man* as the primary source.

[135]Matthew 16:18

[136]Quoted in Walter Oetting, *Church of the Catacombs* (St. Louis: Concordia Publishing House, 1964), p. 80.

[137]This combination of words accounts for the response of the high priest. It's a well-accepted interpretation of the original Greek.

[138]John 5:18

[139]Matthew 23:37

[140]Matthew 9:2

[141]John 6:35

[142]John 5:22

[143]John 8:46

[144]John 9:5

[145]John 14:6

[146]John 8:58

[147]John 8:19

[148]John 12:45

[149]John 12:44

[150]Mark 9:37

[151]John 15:23

[152]John 5:23. John R. W. Stott, *Basic Christianity* (Downers Grove, IL: InterVarsity Press, 1972), p. 26.

[153]Gilbert K. Chesterton, *Orthodoxy*, p. 93.

[154]John 20:17

[155]John 14:2

[156]Genesis 3:11

[157]Don Matzat, *Christ Esteem* (Eugene, OR: Harvest House Publishers, 1990), p. 72.

[158]Isaiah 57:15

[159]2 Corinthians 7:10

[160]2 Corinthians 7:9

[161]Acts 3:19

[162]Matthew 9:2 (NKJV)

[163]Acts 5:31; 11:18

[164]1 Peter 1:8

[165]Hebrews 12:2

[166]Philippians 3:10

[167]Don Matzat, *Christ Esteem,* p. 83.

[168]Ravi Zecharias, *Can Man Live without God,* p. 21.

[169]Psalm 31:5

[170]Romans 1:20

[171]Romans 1:18

[172]Josh McDowell, *The New Evidence That Demands a Verdict,* p. xliii.

[173]John 3:20

[174]1 Corinthians 2:9

[175]2 Peter 1:19

[176]John 14:1

[177]Luke 23:43

[178]John 3:16

[179]Romans 5:20

[180]Romans 6:23

[181]Romans 6:5

[182]Galatians 2:20

[183]Philippians 4:8,9

[184]Joel 1:5,8

[185]Isaiah 30:10,11

[186]This idea is perhaps not unique to Larry Crabb, but I am indebted to him for this and other thoughts in this book.

[187]Paul Little, *Know Why You Believe* (Colorado Springs: Cook Communications, 1999), p. 43.

[188]Josh McDowell, *The New Evidence That Demands a Verdict,* p. 327.

[189]Lee Strobel, *The Case for Faith,* p. 83.

[190]Luke 1:37

[191]Jeremiah 31:3

[192]2 Samuel 12:13

[193]John 20:23

[194]Colossians 3:1

[195]Ephesians 2:6

[196]Colossians 3:1

[197]Larry Crabb, *Finding God* (Grand Rapids: Zondervan Publishing House, 1993), p. 172.

[198]John 15:4

[199]Larry Crabb, *Inside Out* (Colorado Springs: NavPress, 1988), p. 18.

[200]Taken from Acts 7:54-60

[201]Colossians 3:3

[202]John 5:24

[203]Romans 8:19

[204]Often attributed to Martin Luther.

[205]Ephesians 5:25,27

[206]Hebrews 11:38

[207]Revelation 1:18

[208]Revelation 2:4

[209]Revelation 3:16

[210]Revelation 2:10

[211]Matthew 13:35

[212]1 John 4:10

[213]Larry Crabb, *Connecting* (Nashville: Word Publishing Group, 1997), p. 76.

[214]1 John 3:16

[215]1 John 1:4

[216]Philemon 6

[217]Based on Luke 5:1-11